Frame Carpentry

FOR PROS BY PROS®

BUILDER-TESTED | CODE APPROVED

Frame Carpentry

Editors of **Fine Homebuilding**

The Taunton Press

The Taunton Press, Inc., 63 South Main Street, Newtown, CT 06470-2344
e-mail: tp@taunton.com

Editor: Peter Chapman
Copy editor: Carolyn Mandarano
Indexer: Jay Kreider
Interior design: Carol Singer
Cover design: Barbara Cottingham
Layout: Barbara Cottingham, Lynne Phillips
Cover photo: David Frane

Fine Homebuilding® is a trademark of The Taunton Press, Inc., registered in the U.S. Patent and Trademark Office.

The following names/manufacturers appearing in *Frame Carpentry* are trademarks: AdvanTech®, Apple® iTunes®, Bostitch®, Chief Architect®, Cora-A-Vent™, DeGrip-Rite®, DeWalt®, Douglas™, Dumpster®, Duo-Fast®, FastenMaster®, Goof Off®, Google™, Goo Gone®, GreenFiber®, Homasote®, MemBrain™, MicroPro®, Paslode®, Senco®, SilveRboard®, Simpson Strong-Tie®, SketchUp®, Speed® Square, Stanley®, Stanley® Anti-Vibe®, Stiletto®, TiBone™, TimberLOK®, Tremco®, Wolmanized®, Zip System®

Library of Congress Cataloging-in-Publication Data

Names: Taunton Press, author.
Title: Frame carpentry / editors of Fine homebuilding.
Other titles: Fine homebuilding.
Description: Newtown, CT : Taunton Press, Inc., [2019] | Includes index.
Identifiers: LCCN 2018055937 | ISBN 9781641550611
Subjects: LCSH: House framing. | Framing (Building)
Classification: LCC TH2301 .F73 2019 | DDC 694/.2--dc23
LC record available at https://lccn.loc.gov/2018055937

PRINTED IN THE UNITED STATES OF AMERICA
10 9 8 7 6 5 4 3 2 1

This book is compiled from articles that originally appeared in *Fine Homebuilding* magazine. Unless otherwise noted, construction costs listed were current at the time the articles first appeared.

About Your Safety: Homebuilding is inherently dangerous. From accidents with power tools to falls from ladders, scaffolds, and roofs, builders risk serious injury and even death. We try to promote safe work habits throughout this book, but what is safe for one person under certain circumstances may not be safe for you under different circumstances. So don't try anything you learn about here (or elsewhere) unless you're certain that it is safe for you. If something about an operation doesn't feel right, don't do it. Look for another way. Please keep safety foremost in your mind whenever you're working.

ACKNOWLEDGMENTS

Special thanks to the authors, editors, art directors, copy editors, and other staff members of *Fine Homebuilding* who contributed to the development of the articles in this book.

Contents

In Praise of Framers

Framing contractors are among the unsung heroes of homebuilding. They come on site when the ground is still muddy, the electricity and plumbing are still temporary, and there is no shelter from the often harsh elements other than what they create in the course of their job. Their work is some of the most physically demanding of any trade, and their tools among the heaviest to lug. Yet framers don't get anywhere near the glory of, say, interior trim carpenters, kitchen cabinet installers, or the crew installing that new hardwood floor. In fact, for a framer the only reward for a job well done is that his or her work is hardly noticed, because it doesn't cause problems for those that follow. All of the contractors that come next in the building process depend on the forethought of the framer to help make their particular jobs easier. It's up to the framer to set the stage for the electrician, plumber, and drywall installers, each of which has their own needs for access, fastening, and support. It's up to the framer to add blocking in all of the places it might later be needed by stair builders, cabinet installers, and the homeowner who decides, 20 years after the house is completed, that he or she wants a grab bar near the shower. It's up the framer to start level and square—and stay that way from sill plate to ridge—so that joints in molding come together nicely for the finish carpenters.

If you picked up this book, it's because you have a desire to learn how a good framer does this work. I commend you for this, and encourage you to do this, and all homebuilding work, with the same dedication to care and quality that is embodied in each *Fine Homebuilding* author. If you reach the last page of this book and still crave more, I urge you to browse our website, www.finehomebuilding.com, where we have decades' worth of similar content, for framing, and everything that comes before and after in the process of building and remodeling.

Happy building.

—Justin Fink
Editor, *Fine Homebuilding*

Tools and Materials

Outfitting a Tool Belt

BY PATRICK MCCOMBE

I was recently asked what I thought were the essential tools for greenhorn carpenters and what it would cost to buy them. It's a good question. I have my opinions, but so does everybody else who's been in the trenches. I asked several coworkers who are former carpenters, and we developed a list of core carpentry tools—specifically, the tools that a carpenter needs often enough to keep in a tool belt, itself the first item on the list. I then headed to the nearest home center and bought everything on the list, with the goal of keeping the total under $200.

I got my start in carpentry more than 20 years ago, so although some of my choices are decidedly old school, my emphasis was on high-quality, affordable tools. You should feel free to choose tools based on your budget and on what feels right.

When you go tool shopping, buy good stuff, because there's nothing more frustrating than struggling with bad tools. Assuming you don't lose them, you might still be using some of them 20 years from now.

PENCIL, $1. Carpenter's pencils are square so that they won't roll away. Carry two in your belt for when the lead breaks or if you drop one while on a ladder or at another inopportune time. Carry a permanent marker ($1), too.

CAT'S PAW, $15. Modern Japanese-style cat's paws for pulling nails are a vast improvement over traditional styles. I prefer the style with cat's paws on both ends of the tool, but those with both a cat's paw and a pry or molding bar are equally useful.

5

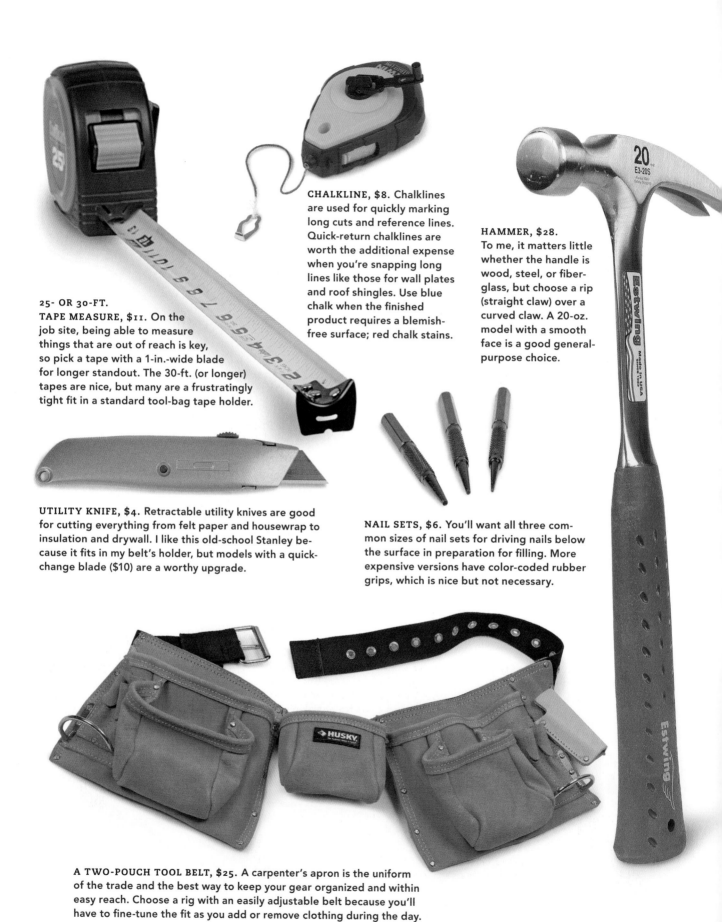

25- OR 30-FT. TAPE MEASURE, $11. On the job site, being able to measure things that are out of reach is key, so pick a tape with a 1-in.-wide blade for longer standout. The 30-ft. (or longer) tapes are nice, but many are a frustratingly tight fit in a standard tool-bag tape holder.

CHALKLINE, $8. Chalklines are used for quickly marking long cuts and reference lines. Quick-return chalklines are worth the additional expense when you're snapping long lines like those for wall plates and roof shingles. Use blue chalk when the finished product requires a blemish-free surface; red chalk stains.

HAMMER, $28. To me, it matters little whether the handle is wood, steel, or fiberglass, but choose a rip (straight claw) over a curved claw. A 20-oz. model with a smooth face is a good general-purpose choice.

UTILITY KNIFE, $4. Retractable utility knives are good for cutting everything from felt paper and housewrap to insulation and drywall. I like this old-school Stanley because it fits in my belt's holder, but models with a quick-change blade ($10) are a worthy upgrade.

NAIL SETS, $6. You'll want all three common sizes of nail sets for driving nails below the surface in preparation for filling. More expensive versions have color-coded rubber grips, which is nice but not necessary.

A TWO-POUCH TOOL BELT, $25. A carpenter's apron is the uniform of the trade and the best way to keep your gear organized and within easy reach. Choose a rig with an easily adjustable belt because you'll have to fine-tune the fit as you add or remove clothing during the day.

DON'T FORGET SAFETY GEAR

WHILE BROWSING THE HAND-TOOL AISLE AT A HOME CENTER, I noticed that relatively little has changed since I outfitted myself more than 20 years ago. One important thing has changed, though: Safety glasses and ear protection are much better than they used to be. I wish I would have listened when people told me to wear hearing protection; my hearing is permanently compromised from noisy equipment and power tools.

DUST MASKS, $8 FOR 2. Skip the cheapest dust masks, which offer little protection, and upgrade to a two-strap model with an N95 rating instead. Wear one whenever you're sanding, scraping, cutting pressure-treated lumber, or doing demo.

HEARING PROTECTION, $8. Band-style ear plugs, which store around your neck, are always ready—although the plastic band breaks far too easily. Disposable foam plugs work well, but handling turns them gross quickly. Washable plugs are another option ($5), but their 25-db. noise reduction offers less protection.

SAFETY GLASSES, $10. Get a pair of both clear and tinted glasses so that you'll be protected in all conditions. If you wear corrective lenses, consider prescription safety glasses (about $200). You'll find it's money well spent when—not if—something happens.

RAFTER SQUARE, $8. Often called a Speed Square, a rafter square is made for marking straight and angled cuts on everything from rafters and joists to trim and siding. Choose one made from thick plastic or aluminum, as thin aluminum versions bend too easily. For another $2.50, you can get a square with a little book filled with rafter tables—probably a good investment.

3-PIECE CHISEL SET, $20. More important than the chisel brand is learning how to keep your chisels sharp (see "Building Skills" in *Fine Homebuilding* #217 and online at FineHomebuilding.com/extras). You'll need only one in your belt for cutting, scraping, and occasional prying, but having a set of ½-, ¾-, and 1-in. widths should mean that at least one is always sharp.

Choosing the Right Framing Nailer

BY MICHAEL SPRINGER

Builders often ask for tool tests of framing nailers, but all the variations on the market make that a tall order to fill. There are stick nailers with 20°-, 28°-, and 30°-magazine angles, not to mention coil nailers. Some tools max out at 3¼-in. nails, some at 3½-in. nails, and some at 4-in. nails or longer. Some tools shoot full round-head nails, clipped-head nails, or both. With the variety of models available from the major pneumatic brands, power-tool companies, and lower-cost clone and private-label manufacturers, the framing-nailer category must represent 100 or more tools.

Here, my goal is to condense all the relevant information about these nailers into a brief guide, highlighting the latest technologies and features these tools have to offer.

It all starts with the nails

Picking a framing nailer starts with knowing the nails you'll be shooting. You want a tool that you can keep supplied with nails easily and affordably. Regional preferences and sometimes even building codes dictate which fasteners—and therefore which tools—are common in your area.

California and other Western states have adopted full round-head nailers, while most of the rest of the country relies on clipped-head models. Specific code requirements have driven some of the divide, but these geographic tool preferences can be traced back to where the big nailer companies started, or at least to the regional markets where their distribution was originally focused. Think Bostitch in New England, Hitachi in the West, and Paslode and Senco in between. As the major players staked their claims, whatever type of nail their early tools required became the default favorite in the territory.

Regardless of nail type, follow the nailing schedule for each material, component, and assembly you construct as specified by the building code covering your area. Model building codes were written for hand-driven nails, so they specify only the size, spacing, and number of nails used for specific connections and applications, not the type of head. The International Code Council's ESR-1539 report—which is free and widely available online—is written with an awareness of pneumatic nailers and is a good place to find the details of nailed connections (and equivalent connections) required to meet all the model building codes.

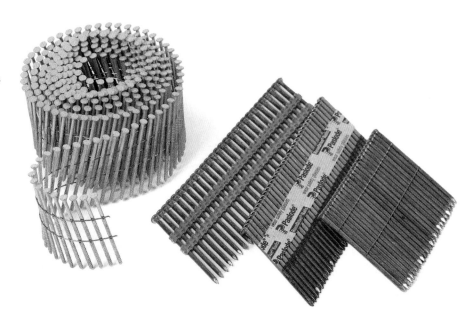

NARROWING THIS BROAD MARKET starts with a decision about which nails you'll be shooting.

Know your nails

Framing nailers come in two styles: coil or stick. Coil nailers have an adjustable canister that accepts a coil of nails strung together by two rows of thin wire welded to the shanks of the nails. These nails have a full round head. Stick nailers fit two angled sticks of 25 to 40 nails collated with wire, paper, or plastic, with the head of each nail nested just above the head of the nail in front of it. The style of nail head is usually based on the collation angle.

NAIL HEADS

Full round-head nails are acceptable everywhere in the United States and for every type of framing connection. They are also typically available in thicker shank diameters. The downside is that nail heads take up space in a magazine, so you get fewer nails per stick.

MAXIMUM NAIL DIAMETER

Nailers also have limitations to the maximum diameter of compatible fasteners they can accept. The minimum nail thickness for wall sheathing isn't typically the same as the minimum nail thickness for rafters. This varies by region, though, and also can change based on what the architect or engineer has specified in the building plans. I know a framer

in the Southwest who is allowed to use 3-in. by 0.131-in. (10d) nails for everything—an easy task for any framing nailer.

MAXIMUM NAIL LENGTH

Some brands have created a new compact-framer category, designed to be lighter and to fit more easily between 16-in.-on-center framing layouts. The

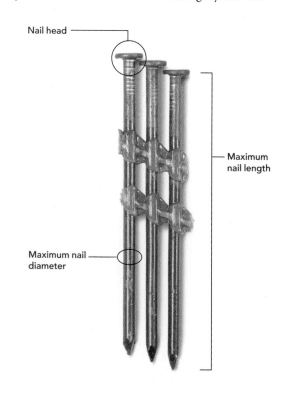

Nail head

Maximum nail length

Maximum nail diameter

dividing line for this category is typically maximum nail length—3¼ in. for compact models, 3½ in. for full size—but the maximum shank thickness also may differ by collation angle and brand.

The maximum size is often referenced in a nailer's model number. For instance, a domestic model number may express maximum nail lengths of 3¼ in. and 3½ in. as 325 and 350. Foreign models may use 83 and 90, which are the lengths in millimeters.

It's worth noting that some compact nailers don't have the guts to shoot into dense engineered lumber well. Even if the longest nails you shoot are 3¼ in., you may be better off with a full-size nailer because of its superior power.

TWO HEAD-STYLE OPTIONS FOR PAPER-COLLATED STICK NAILS

Depending on your region and applicable codes, the type of head on your nails is a big deal, and the head style is usually tied to the collation angle. There are a few variations.

Clipped head At steeper collation angles (28° and 30°), manufacturers can pack nails closer together by clipping off one side of the head. The resulting D-shape has less surface area than round heads of the same diameter and causes these nails to be

Clipped head

disallowed for some applications. Some of the nails are called notched instead of clipped because the chunk removed from their heads is rounded instead of straight.

Offset round head Available in both 28° and 30° angles, these nails provide the code compliance of a

Offset round head

full round-head nail with the tight spacing common to a stick of clipped-head nails.

Must-have features for a quality framing nailer

Even an occasional user needs a competent tool. Here are some important features to consider when choosing a nailer.

Balance and feel are important to your overall comfort and the control of the tool. Before you plunk down cash, be sure to fill the tool with nails and to hang a hose off the back to evaluate how it really feels. Otherwise, you're just kicking the tires.

The body of the nailer will be either aluminum or magnesium, and the choice is a bit of a toss-up. Magnesium is lighter but more brittle, and it costs more than standard aluminum, which is heavier and more durable. It's best just to go with how the tool feels overall, though. I don't know that anyone buys a nailer based on the material it's cast from.

A selective-fire setting lets you switch the tool from sequential-fire (single-shot) mode to bump-fire mode. The best designs are tool free, but because most users never switch back to sequential fire, replacing or adjusting the trigger assembly once is not a big deal. If you plan to switch back and forth, opt for a nailer that has a toggle switch.

Top-load versus rear-load magazines is a decision you will have to make. For myself and the guys I know, the answer is unanimously in favor of rear load. Hanging the tool down with one hand lets you load in a more comfortable position; the spring-

FRAMING NAILERS: COIL OR STICK?

COIL NAILERS

Coil nailers have an adjustable canister that accepts a coil of nails—up to 200 framing nails or 300 sheathing nails at a time—angled at 15° and strung together by two rows of thin wire welded to the shanks of the nails. In most areas of the United States, these nailers are far less popular than stick nailers, but they are common in areas of the Northeast and in a few pockets of Louisiana, Missouri, and Texas. Interestingly, this is what the rest of the world considers a framing nailer.

PROS
- These tools shoot a lot of nails between reloading, potentially saving time.
- The tools' compact size provides some accessibility advantages.
- If a model fits shorter nails and has a protective nose-piece, it can double as a high-volume siding or trim nailer.

CONS
- When fully loaded with hundreds of nails, these tools can be heavy and unwieldy.
- Dropping or bending a coil of nails often renders it unusable and creates expensive waste.

NOTABLE BRANDS
Bostitch, DeWalt, Grip-Rite, Hitachi, Makita, Max, PneuTools, Senco

STICK NAILERS

Plastic-collated nailers fit round-head nails collated between 20° and 22°. A stiff collating strip—typically plastic but also available in rigid paper—allows enough space for full-size heads with the nails situated side-by-side. Two sticks of nails fit in the magazine for a load of about 60 nails. Full round-head nails have been a necessity in some parts of California for a while, so these tools are particularly big on the West Coast and in much of the West in general.

20° to 22°

PROS
- Round-head nails are allowed for every connection type, so these tools can be used anywhere in the United States with their standard fasteners. (Some codes require the use of round-head nails only.)
- Round-head nails are typically available in larger shank sizes than other types.
- The easier manufacturing of plastic-collated nail sticks makes them significantly less expensive than the paper- or wire-collated nails used in other nailers.

CONS
- Nails of the standard plastic-collated variety spew out bits of plastic shrapnel, which is a nuisance when they ricochet off the wall into your face or leave the floor dotted with scattered shards.
- The long, low magazine keeps the nose of the tool from fitting into tight spots as easily as higher-angle stick nailers.

Wire-weld-collated nailers have their own specific collation angle and their own specific homegrown market. These tools started strong in the Northeast and have stayed strong, with 80% of their sales in New England. Overall, the 28° tools are similar to the 30° type (they share the same pros and cons), but 28° clipped-head nails are typically collated with thin wires tack-welded to the side of the nails. Plastic-collated and paper-tape versions of 28° nails can be found, even some with round heads, but before you bring one out to build shear walls in California, make sure you can get fasteners for it. These tools are largely unknown in much of the country, and their diet of special fasteners may not be on the menu far from home.

Paper-collated nailers have magazine angles anywhere from 30° to 35°, but the fasteners they fit are usually referred to as 30° nails. These tools are known generically as clipped-head nailers or paper-tape nailers. Standard clipped-head nails for these tools are collated with paper tape glued along the sides of nails that are packed shank to shank. Magazines typically fit two sticks of these densely packed nails, providing about 80 nails.

PROS
- The steep magazine angle of the tool affords its nose the deepest reach into corners.
- Tighter packed sticks of nails hold significantly more fasteners per load than the sticks in full round-head nailers.

CONS
- Clipped-head nails are not approved for structural connections in some areas, so more specialized offset round-head nails may be needed.
- These tools require more expensive fasteners than full round-head nailers.

NOTABLE BRANDS
Plastic-collated: Bosch, Bostitch, DeWalt, Duo-Fast, Grip-Rite, Hitachi, Makita, Max, PneuTools, Senco.
Wire-weld-collated: Bostitch, Grip-Rite, Hitachi, Max.
Paper-collated: Bosch, Bostitch, DeWalt, Grip-Rite, Hitachi, Max, Paslode, PneuTools, Senco.

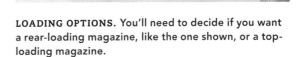

LOADING OPTIONS. You'll need to decide if you want a rear-loading magazine, like the one shown, or a top-loading magazine.

loaded follower can't accidentally slam into the nails and damage the collation strip; the remaining nails can't fall out as soon as you release the follower; and having the follower engaged when loading new nails keeps the last few remaining nails tightly in place so that they won't cause a jam.

Depth-of-drive adjustment is important for meeting building codes, and the best setups work without the need for tools. Without this feature, you have to adjust the regulator on the air compressor when you switch from LVL headers to nailing off sheathing. It's not worth compromising on this feature.

HANDY UPGRADES
Whether you're framing on a regular basis or just looking for some extra perks, try these features.

A few manufacturers are using **nose magnets** to hold the last few nails in a stick firmly in place when reloading the magazine. This is a simple, useful addition to help make the reloading process goofproof.

Built-in air filters are a welcome addition to keep unwanted gunk out of a nailer's innards. Pads of filter media are useful enough, but the best filters are self-cleaning cartridges that cough out any trapped particles every time you unplug the air hose.

A nonmarring nose cap allows your framing nailer to become a siding, trim, or deck nailer. Without a cap, the teeth on the nose turn cedar or redwood into hamburger.

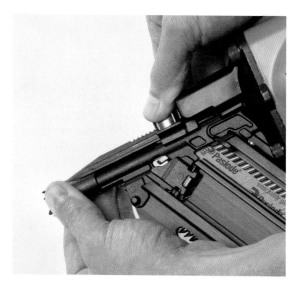

AVOID DAMAGE. A nonmarring nose cap protects your wood.

FEATURES FOR PRODUCTION FRAMERS

- **A rafter hook** for keeping your nailer close at hand is a must if you don't want your tool to slow you down. The lack of a hook is not a deal breaker, however. Aftermarket hooks that connect at the air fitting are available and may be preferable to a factory-installed hook that is clumsy or too small.
- **Toenailing spikes** (see photo at right) that really grab are the key to fast, accurate toenailing. Look for a nose with especially sharp spikes protruding well out from the sides.
- **Real-world durability and longevity** are hard to test. Many top brands have legacy tools that have been in production for decades, so talk to other guys in the field. Check local tool-repair shops, too. They might not be able to tell you which nailer will last, but they sure can tell you which ones break.

Specialty Levels

BY DON BURGARD

Needing to find level and plumb is basic to just about every aspect of building and remodeling. While the market for laser levels continues to grow, you can still find a variety of spirit levels on most job sites. Not all spirit levels are long and straight, however. Inventive minds have discovered that a small container filled with colored liquid and a bubble can be incorporated into a variety of designs, each of which can offer an easier and sometimes more accurate way to get a reading.

Bull's-eye level and cross-check level

The bubble in a bull's-eye level floats inside a convex disk instead of a cylindrical vial. Level is achieved when the bubble finds the bull's-eye in the center of the disk. A bull's-eye level is useful when placing items such as large appliances that need to be level in two directions. The cross-check level provides the same information, but it does so with two cylindrical vials at a right angle to each other. When the bubbles in both vials are centered, the object the device is resting on is level.

COUNTERCLOCKWISE FROM TOP LEFT:
Bull's-eye level; cross-check level; line level; torpedo level; post level.

Line level

This tiny level attaches to a taut stringline and is used to find level for two points on a span. Its degree of accuracy is not precise, and it can't be used for finding level across the entire span (even the tightest stringline will sag a little), but it's good enough to use for projects such as setting fence posts, checking the pitch of a driveway, or ensuring a level retaining wall. The trick is to position the level in the center of the string. The farther the tool is from the center, the less accurate your reading will be.

Post level

Made of plastic and either hinged or molded into a 90° angle, a post level is attached with a rubber band or elastic strap. It registers plumb with a center vial and level with a vial on each side of the angle. While its design makes it ideal for fitting around posts, a post level can also be attached to a large-diameter pipe.

Torpedo level

Designed to fit into tight spaces, torpedo levels pack a lot of features into a small package. Usually about 8 in. to 10 in. long, most of these levels have at least three vials: one each for level, plumb, and 45°-angle measurements. Some include a fourth vial for measuring 22.5° or 30° angles. Rare-earth magnets along one edge of many torpedo levels keep the level from moving when it's against ferrous metal. Some manufacturers groove this edge so that it fits better around pipes. If you carry a torpedo level with magnets in your tool belt, however, you may find it annoying to have to scrape away bits of steel from fasteners and drill shavings.

Manufacturers have customized torpedo levels to a remarkable extent. Johnson, for example, has 17 different torpedo levels listed on its website. One of them is designed for welders, two have luminescent vials, and one has a thumbscrew for attaching to a pipe before bending an angle.

VIRTUAL BUBBLES

IF THERE'S A SMARTPHONE IN YOUR POCKET, you already have a multipurpose leveling tool; you just need to download any one of many apps offered in both the Google Play and Apple iTunes stores. These apps display a virtual vial and bubble, but they also calculate angles to one or two decimal points. Many apps display both cylindrical and circular vials and automatically toggle between the two depending on whether the phone is on edge or lying flat. Don't trust a smartphone app to give you a reading that's as accurate as what you can get from a tool designed specifically for that purpose, however.

The Rich History of Hammer Design

BY AARON FAGAN

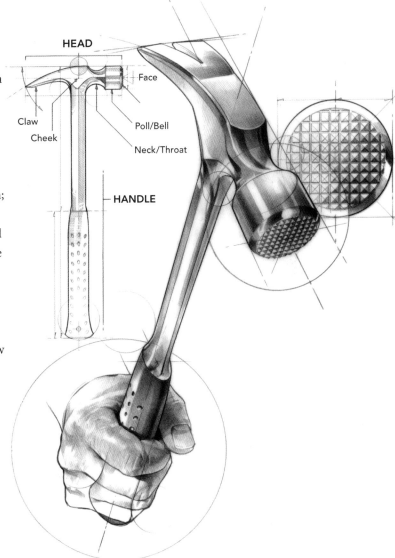

HEAD

Claw

Cheek

Face

Poll/Bell

Neck/Throat

HANDLE

The first nail I ever drove was with my father's hammer—a True Temper A16 Rocket, which he had won in a nailing contest at an annual picnic for the hardware dealers of Rochester, N.Y., in 1963. His instruction to me that day sounded quite simple. He said, "It's all about letting the hammer do the work." I am certain that, like anyone wielding a hammer for the first time, I must have made a rather sad scene: There I am, holding the hammer too tightly, my hand and arm singing with vibration; choked too high on the handle; missing, repeatedly; the bent nail mirroring my defeat with its head slumped down; and, ultimately, that ancient rite, the Dance of the Purple Thumb.

That was 30 years ago, and the art of letting the hammer do the work is one I will not master. Still, my story illustrates that hammers, and our history with them, are personal to us. The carpenters I know think that their hammer is the best hammer, and they are happy to tell you why. But hammers, too, have a story to tell. Their designs have evolved over the millennia, always moving us closer to that goal: letting them do the work.

Still building Rome

We humans have had some time to think about hammers. Even in the Stone Age, there was great sophistication in choosing the right stone for the job, and much later, the right stick, bone, or antler to tie the stone to with sinew or other materials. But it was not until the Roman Empire that a nailing hammer emerged. Dating from the first century, it had a wood handle attached to a metal head with a striking surface on one side, and a split, curved claw for pulling nails on the other. The Romans made extensive use of nails for construction, and it's a legacy that persists in our nail-sizing system: The "d" stands for the Roman coin denarius, which was presumably worth ten donkeys. Nails were priced per hundred, so one hundred 8d nails was equal to 80 donkeys. At that cost, the ability to extract and reuse those nails seems self-evident.

For centuries afterward, the head and the handle underwent countless interpretations from blacksmith to blacksmith, but these were slight modifications from that Roman design. While the use of steel for hammerheads is thought to date back to the Romans, the widespread use of hickory for handles did not occur until the mid-19th century in America. (Hickory is unique for its strength, density, and excellent shock resistance.) From the beginning of the tool's history, the single greatest design challenge was keeping the head securely affixed to the handle.

Revolutionaries

Around 1840, a carpenter in a small crew hired to build a church in Norwich, N.Y., realized he had left his hammer back home. The local blacksmith was David Maydole, who had been experimenting with hammer designs. (Even though the Industrial Revolution was newly underway in the United States, hammers still came from blacksmiths.) Maydole was frustrated by the tendency for hammerheads to fly off, and he tried to do something about it. Inspired by the extended eye of an adz—a tool similar to an ax—he added a tapered neck to wedge the handle inside the head, resulting in the adz-eye hammer.

DON'T FLY OFF THE HANDLE

WHILE DAVID MAYDOLE'S ADZ-EYE HAMMER better secured the head to the hickory handle, handles still broke, requiring a tedious replacement. Todd Coonrad's Douglas design offers both overstrike protection and the ability to more readily change the handle.

Douglas DFR-2016
Head: stainless steel
Handle: hickory
Weight: 20 oz.

As the story goes, the carpenter was so happy with Maydole's hammer that the rest of his crew decided to order it. Word spread, the local store ordered some, and a New York City tool merchant placed a standing order with Maydole for as many hammers as he could make. Though Maydole never patented his adz-eye hammer, in 1845 he founded the David Maydole Hammer Co., which grew to be one of the largest hammer manufacturers in the U.S.

THE HAMMER THAT HOLDS THE NAIL

HENRY CHENEY WAS THE FIRST TO CONCEIVE A HAMMER with a nail starter in the head, a feature that is nearly standard on modern tools such as this DeWalt, a lightweight steel hammer that gives titanium tools a run for their money.

DeWalt DWHT51135

Head: steel
Handle: steel
Weight: 14 oz.

ously marketed as the "world's standard since 1836." This would have meant that Cheney started making this hammer when he was 15 years old. In addition, Cheney's patented design was for cut nails, whereas the Cheney Nailer's nail starter required wire nails, which didn't come into standard use until 1910.

Cheney's conception of a "hammer that holds the nail"—however indirectly—is at work today in the many modern hammers with a magnetic nail-starting feature.

DO ME A SOLID

IN 1926, ERNEST ESTWING IN-TRODUCED a virtually indestructible, forged hammer made from a single piece of solid carbon steel with a lac-quered grip made of stacked leather rings. In 2001, Mark Martinez began selling the TiBone, the first solid-titanium, lightweight framing hammer.

Stiletto TB15MC

Head: titanium
Handle: titanium
Weight: 15 oz.

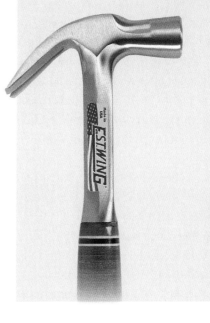

In Fly Creek, N.Y., a mere 40 miles away from Maydole's operation, another inventor, Henry Cheney, introduced a nail-starting system near the claw, which he patented in 1871. That, however, is not the design that made his name famous. The popular Cheney Nailer was introduced in 1927, a full 50 years after Henry Cheney's death. That hammer was based on a modified patent by Arthur Taylor and Scott Hinman of Elyria, Ohio, and was disingenu-

And just as the essence of the Roman claw hammer has endured, so too has Maydole's adz-eye hammer.

The head/handle problem was revisited in 1926 by Ernest Estwing, who introduced a virtually indestructible, forged hammer made from a single piece of solid carbon steel with a lacquered grip made of stacked leather rings. Estwing's design was one of many as a new age of invention dawned. Countless inventors flooded the U.S. Patent and Trademark Office with ingenious modifications and interpretations of the tool.

Postwar promise and the age of science

Hammers are a time capsule containing a compression of history. For example, four-clawed hammers, designed to reduce damage in extracting costly nails for reuse, became popular during the Great Depression. After World War II, a booming economy and new fascination with science meant that hammers would be designed in a completely different way.

During the 1950s, a growing middle class was realizing the promise of the American Dream for the first time, leading to an unprecedented demand for housing. This ushered in a period of reimagining the hammer to meet those demands. Rather than a single crew building one house from start to finish, there emerged framing crews, whose sole charge was to get a house framed quickly and accurately for finish crews to complete. The common hammer—with its short handle, smooth face, and curved claw—had exhausted its potential in this setting and came to be classed as a finish hammer, to be used for tasks less intensive than rough carpentry. Framing became a task for what is now known as the California framing hammer.

Framing hammers began as rigging hatchets, which were the primary tools workers in California used to make wood oil derricks before World War II. A rigging-hatchet head has an ax blade on one side and a short-necked milled hammer face on the other. It is balanced, grabs nails well, and has a heavy head weight for lots of striking power. It has a long hickory handle that is either straight or curved with an adz eye or a teardrop-shape (single-bit) eye. For many carpenters, the downside of using a rigging hatchet for home building was the dangerous blade (unions banned them) and the tool's inability to extract nails efficiently. Crews began replacing the blade with the claws from old hammers. The late Larry Haun, after he had seen a modified hatchet on the job, had his first one made in 1954. The legendary carpenter wrote about this in 2006: "I took my Plumb rigging hatchet home and cut off the blade with a hacksaw. I had an old Estwing hammer that supplied the claws. I took the pieces to a friend who had an electric arc welder in his garage, and he put the parts together. Although my hammer was a rough-looking tool, it was now safer to use, and I could drive framing nails easily with one lick. The straight-claw, long-handle California framer was born."

Bob Hart, a Los Angeles framing contractor, was one of the first to manufacture these hammers. He began his business by selling his hammers to lumberyards out of the trunk of his car. The popularity of California framing hammers grew through exemplary designs by such makers as Vaughan and Dalluge, and now virtually every manufacturer offers some version of the tool.

Where job-site ingenuity created the California framing hammer, 20th-century science sought to remedy the shortcomings of the solid-steel hammer. Although these hammers were an incredibly strong alternative to wood hammers and were better for pulling nails, they were heavy and provided very little shock absorption. Until this time, little, if any, consideration had been given to the end user. Most previous innovations did not go much beyond getting a hammer to drive a nail without breaking. Arm fatigue, the amount of force expended, and comfort were only of peripheral concern.

In 1955, Plumb introduced the first hammers with fiberglass handles as an alternative to wood or steel. The same year, True Temper introduced the Rocket my father would win in 1963, which boasted a steel-

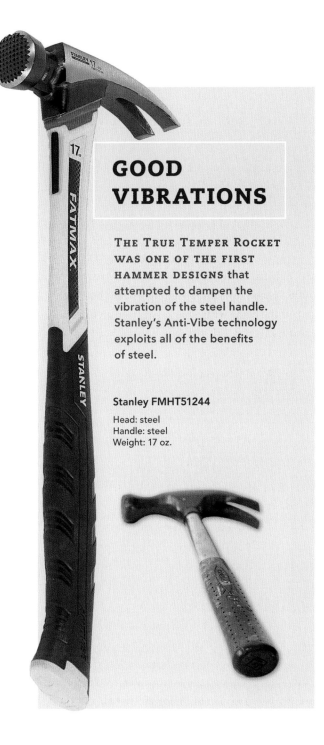

GOOD VIBRATIONS

THE TRUE TEMPER ROCKET WAS ONE OF THE FIRST HAMMER DESIGNS that attempted to dampen the vibration of the steel handle. Stanley's Anti-Vibe technology exploits all of the benefits of steel.

Stanley FMHT51244

Head: steel
Handle: steel
Weight: 17 oz.

smooth or milled faces. This period saw the rise of many new hammer designs and materials and also introduced new avenues for refining and building on that progress.

Clash of the titans

As the study of ergonomics matured, researchers could measure how hammers actually work and then develop ways to change them. For example, they were now able to determine the force required to grip a hammer and to understand the way a hammer distributes force when it strikes; this in turn helped them find ways to curb vibration, increase striking velocity, and optimize the sweet spot on the hammer's face. This continuing quest for a better tool shows how far we have come in our story from rocks tied to sticks, but also how little has changed. A hammer's primary function is still about driving nails and extracting them, but there are other functions a hammer needs to do just as well. A hammer needs to pry boards apart and knock elements into alignment. It's also one of the principal tools for demolition work. Each role calls for specifications no single hammer contains. In an attempt to address as many of these roles as possible, manufacturers in the late 1990s introduced materials such as titanium, graphite, and carbon fiber, and features such as side nail pulls, magnetic nail starters, and interchangeable (milled or smooth) faces.

Because you can swing it faster, a hammer with a titanium head can work just as well as one with a steel head. A titanium hammer transfers 98% of the energy from swinging the hammer to the nail, and does so with dramatically less shock than a steel hammer, which transfers only 70% of that energy to the nail. The two principal complaints are that titanium is five times as expensive as steel, and that titanium hammers are cast as opposed to forged. Stiletto Hammers does offer a removable steel face, which serves several purposes. Steel makes a more durable face than titanium, but the face can also be switched from milled to smooth or replaced when it wears down.

tube handle with a rubberized grip. Hammers such as these signaled the dawn of products marketed as utilizing "space-age technology." Their handles were designed to be shock resistant, ergonomic, stronger than wood, and lighter than solid steel. They were still on the heavy side, however, and did not provide the clarity of sensation that nailing with a wood handle offers. Hammerheads were now being offered with either curved or straight (rip) claws and

A nearly standard feature on modern hammers is a magnetic nail starter at the front of the hammer, which was first introduced in 1995 on a production-made framing hammer designed by Mark Martinez. In 1999, after acquiring the Stiletto trademark and production rights, he began selling the first titanium-head framing hammer. In 2001, he produced the first solid-titanium hammer, called the TiBone.

DeWalt, owned by Stanley Black & Decker, makes a 14-oz. hammer designed to deliver the striking power of a 28-oz. hammer. To add strength, the hammer is made by MIG-welding two forged pieces of steel together. Stanley has a long history of putting end-user feedback to use in its hammer designs and has made fervent innovation a central part of its design strategies. The company's innovations include graphite handles, shock reduction in its steel hammers through its Anti-Vibe design, and grips with grooves for sweat to run off.

Possibly the height of aesthetic and functional design in the hammer so far comes from Todd Coonrad. He has a background in industrial design, but it was through his work as a contractor that he began to question and reimagine the hammer. Like many carpenters, Coonrad preferred hickory handles but grew tired of replacing broken ones. In 1995, he developed a unique head-to-handle assembly that not only allows handles to be changed more readily, but, by creating a channel in the handle for the head to slide into, offers overstrike protection, increasing the longevity of the handle. The steel head features both a magnetic nail starter and a side nail pull. Coonrad has had-licensing agreements with several manufacturers over the years including Hart, Vaughan, and Dalluge, but now he also produces his impeccably crafted hammers through his own company, Douglas (photo, p. 18).

Despite all of this innovation—from the prehistoric discovery of a better striking rock, to Maydole's more secure hammerhead, to today's ergonomic wonders—one truth of hammer design has remained constant: The form of a claw hammer expresses a powerful metaphor of our human ability to revise and create. There is forgiveness of the past in the claw, and hope for the future in its face.

BEST HAMMER YOU'VE EVER OWNED?

We asked the question on *Fine Homebuilding's* "Breaktime" forum, and readers responded:

"I've only owned about four different hammers, but the Stiletto TiBone Mini-14 I have now is my favorite. It weighs less on your belt, swats nails easily whether you're swinging normally or upside down and left-handed, and has a replaceable steel face to make it 'new' again and a soft-rubber handle so your arm doesn't get jarred."

—Waters

"I like the leather handle of the Estwing for the cool factor, but I set it aside and pick up the nylon-handled one for everyday use. The main reason for using the nylon one is that once I sanded off the embossed weight/model info on the butt of the handle, it made a nice rubber mallet to bump things into position, snug things up, etc."

—AichKay

"I love my 14-oz. Stiletto curved handle. That said, the true winner of the personality contest is my True Temper Rocket, straight claw. At 40 years old, it's still part of my daily arsenal."

—KenHill3

Nails

BY DEBRA JUDGE SILBER

Considering how critical nails are to holding wood-frame houses together, it's surprising that we don't pay more attention to them. The fact is, nails and the connections they make are critical to managing building loads and ensuring a safe, durable structure. Although there are many types of nailed connections used in home building, the three basic wood-to-wood connections here illustrate how nails perform.

In service, nails must resist withdrawal forces and shear (lateral) forces; they must also be resistant to pull-through and to combined (off-axis) forces. How well they perform is dependent on the characteristics of the nail, the wood, and the angle at which the nail is driven. Altering these factors—such as using a ring-shank nail or driving the nail at an angle—has a much greater effect on withdrawal resistance than on shear resistance, which is more dependent on the bending strength of the nail and the bearing capacity of the wood surrounding it. Penetration is also important. The rule of thumb is that at least two-thirds of the nail should extend into the base material. So a 1x3 should be fastened to a 4x4 with a 2½-in. (8d) nail, with ¾ in. of the nail going through the 1x3 and 1¾ in. going into the 4x4.

So the next time you swing a hammer, consider this: There's a lot riding on that nail. Here's how it works.

Anatomy of a nail

Head Head size and structure vary with a nail's type and purpose: to avoid overpenetration of the nailed material (such as the broad thin head of a roofing nail) or to embed the head in it (such as the barrel-shaped head of a finishing nail). Embossed nail heads enhance paint adhesion. Head shape has little bearing on withdrawal, but a small head can result in pull-through under force.

Size The size of nails for wood-to-wood applications is commonly referred to by pennyweight. The term is attributed to the original price per hundred nails and is designated with a "d" (for the Roman coin denarius). Pennyweight identifies nails by size on an established but somewhat arbitrary scale (p. 24) and is not considered the best method of specification. Both shank length and diameter can vary slightly among different nails of the same pennyweight: For example, an 8d common nail measures 2½ in. with a 0.131-in. dia., an 8d box nail measures 2½ in. with a 0.113-in. dia., and an 8d sinker nail measures 2⅜ in. with a 0.113-in. dia.

Material Typically made from carbon-steel wire, nails also can be made from aluminum, brass, nickel, bronze, copper, and stainless steel. These materials have different friction values and bending strengths, influencing withdrawal and shear capacity.

NAIL ANATOMY

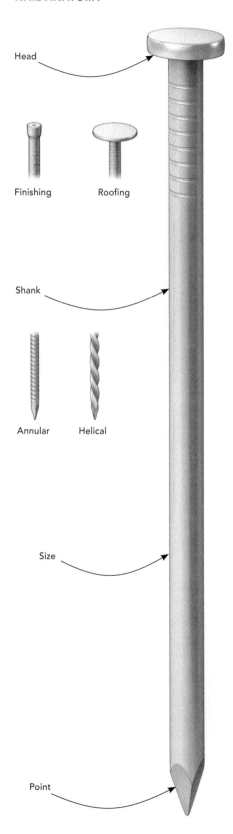

Head

Finishing   Roofing

Shank

Annular   Helical

Size

Point

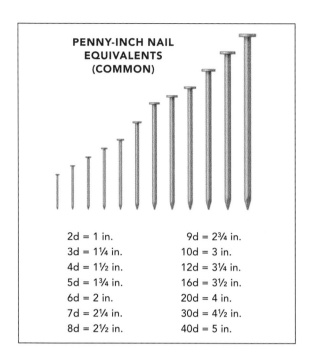

PENNY-INCH NAIL EQUIVALENTS (COMMON)

2d = 1 in.	9d = 2¾ in.
3d = 1¼ in.	10d = 3 in.
4d = 1½ in.	12d = 3¼ in.
5d = 1¾ in.	16d = 3½ in.
6d = 2 in.	20d = 4 in.
7d = 2¼ in.	30d = 4½ in.
8d = 2½ in.	40d = 5 in.

Point Most nails have a four-sided diamond point to make driving easier. Sharp points enhance withdrawal resistance, but they can cause wood to split. Blunt points prevent splitting but lessen withdrawal resistance.

Coating Sacrificial galvanized (zinc) coatings delay corrosion of steel nails. Hot-dipped galvanized nails are immersed in molten zinc to produce a durable coating; other processes include mechanical galvanization and electrogalvanization. Polymer coatings increase initial withdrawal resistance by increasing friction between the nail and the wood. Driving into hardwoods can remove this coating, however.

Shank Smooth-shank nails drive into and pull out of most woods more easily than deformed-shank nails, but those deformations—for example, annular rings or helical threads—can improve holding in certain materials such as hardwoods or plywoods. Ring-shank nails can have up to twice the withdrawal capacity of smooth-shank nails.

Gauge/diameter Gauge is a measure of nail-shank diameter most commonly associated with collated nails. The larger the diameter, the lower the gauge. In general, nails with a large diameter have greater resistance to withdrawal and lateral loads.

THREE BASIC CONNECTIONS

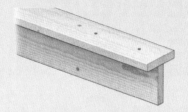

End-nailed connections join two wood members whose grain direction is perpendicular. These connections are easy to make, but they offer little withdrawal resistance (up to 75% less than a nail driven perpendicular to the grain) and effectively resist only shear (lateral) forces.

Face-nailed connections join wood members with the grains parallel. In this application, the nails resist withdrawal, shear, and sometimes off-axis forces.

Toenailed connections offer both withdrawal and shear resistance regardless of the grain direction of the members being nailed. Tests show that these connections are made strongest by using the largest nail that will not cause splitting, by inserting the nail one-third of its length from the joint, by driving the nail at a 30° angle, and by burying the full shank of the nail without causing excessive damage to the wood. When driving several nails, cross-slant driving is somewhat more effective than driving the nails parallel.

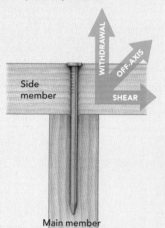

WITHDRAWAL
OFF-AXIS
SHEAR

Side member

Main member

The bottom of the head should press on the side member but not be driven deeper than the head thickness.

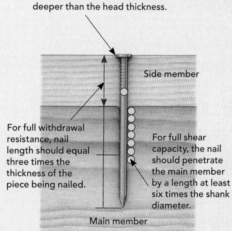

Side member

For full withdrawal resistance, nail length should equal three times the thickness of the piece being nailed.

For full shear capacity, the nail should penetrate the main member by a length at least six times the shank diameter.

Main member

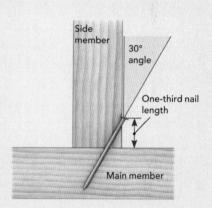

Side member

30° angle

One-third nail length

Main member

OTHER NAILED CONNECTIONS

Dovetail nailing
Nails are driven at an angle through the face of a board to clamp the boards together and to provide better withdrawal resistance than perpendicular face-nailing.

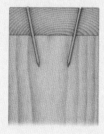

Blind nailing This connection is used with tongue-and-groove boards. Nails are driven at a 45° angle, enabling the groove of the adjacent board to fit over the nail.

Clinch nailing
An extralong nail is driven through the wood members being joined, and the tip is then bent and nailed flush for extra withdrawal resistance.

Framing Lumber: Moisture Content, Species, and Grade

BY DON BURGARD

Engineers, architects, and builders need to know that the framing lumber they specify and install is strong enough to handle the loads placed on it. At the same time, they want to build cost-effectively, which involves knowing when a more expensive species or grade of lumber is unnecessary. For these reasons, each piece of framing lumber has a stamp that contains several pieces of information, three of which—moisture content, species, and grade—are essential to know before you start building.

Moisture content

What it says: Moisture content is identified by one of many abbreviations: AD (air-dried to a moisture level at or below 19%); S-DRY (surfaced dry; that is, the board when surfaced at the mill had a moisture level at or below 19%); S-GRN (surfaced green; that is, the moisture level when the board was surfaced was higher than 19%); KD (kiln-dried at or below 19%); and KD-HT (same as KD, although heat-treated as well to kill pests and fungi). KD-15 and MC-15 lumber have moisture levels of 15% or less.

Why it matters: Some builders choose lumber with a higher moisture level for new construction.

It's cheaper, it's less prone to splitting when nailed, and all the wood will shrink at a similar pace as it dries. Others prefer drier lumber to avoid problems related to shrinkage, such as twisting and nail pops. For remodels, however, go with the drier stuff because it will integrate better with the already dried and shrunken existing lumber. Be aware, however, that moisture content is measured at the mill, not at the lumberyard, so time sitting in rainy weather or hot sun isn't considered.

Species

What it says: Common wood-species stamps include D Fir (Douglas fir), Hem (hemlock), and PP (Ponderosa pine). Abbreviations are sometimes grouped for species with similar characteristics, such as SPF (spruce, pine, and fir) and Hem-Fir (hemlock and fir).

Why it matters: Species can depend on region, but high-strength lumber often is more expensive. That said, it isn't always necessary to use the strongest lumber available. Building codes specify maximum allowable spans for each species, so before buying expensive lumber, check local codes to see if a cheaper species could work.

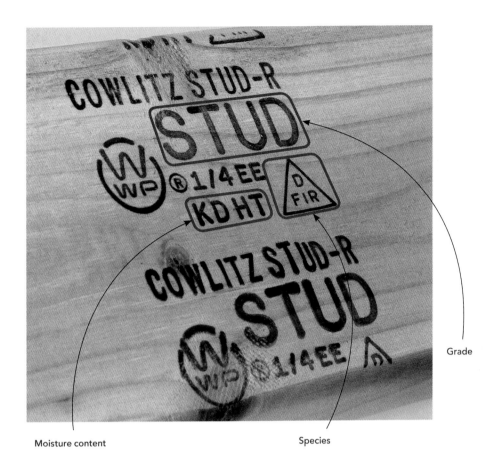

Moisture content

Species

Grade

Grade

What it says: There are four categories of framing lumber, most of which have a hierarchy of grades corresponding to their level of weakening characteristics such as knots, splits, or wane.

STRUCTURAL LIGHT FRAMING
These pieces have the highest strength values and are suitable for use in engineered applications such as trusses, rafters, and joists. They are broken down into four subcategories: select structural, No. 1, No. 2, and No. 3.

LIGHT FRAMING
These pieces can be used as plates, cripples, blocking, and in other areas where high strength isn't crucial. They break down as construction, standard, and utility.

STUD
These pieces are strong enough to handle vertical loads, but they aren't approved for other uses. No subcategories here.

STRUCTURAL JOISTS AND PLANKS
These larger boards have the same grades as structural light framing.

Why it matters: The farther down the hierarchy you go for each category of lumber, the lower the quality and performance of the wood. Because different species have different strength values, grade must be considered hand-in-hand with species. For example, a 10-ft. Douglas-fir 2x4 of a certain grade will have a different strength value than a Ponderosa-pine 2x4 of the same size and grade. The most important thing to remember here is that within the same species, you can always use a piece of lumber graded above what is required for a particular application, but not one that is graded below.

Pressure-Treated Lumber: Preservatives and Retention

BY DON BURGARD

Until 2004, pressure-treated wood for residential use was preserved with chromate copper arsenate (CCA), and the level of treatment was generally the same for all lumber. Because of concerns over arsenic's toxicity, CCA has since been replaced for residential use by a host of preservatives, some of which have themselves been replaced by even newer formulations. Compared to CCA, these preservatives contain higher amounts of copper, which is expensive, so manufacturers produce pressure-treated lumber with different retention levels.

Retention level measures how much of the preservative is retained in the wood after the pressure treatment ends. It's expressed in pounds per cubic foot (lb. per cu. ft.) of wood fiber. The higher the retention level, the better equipped the wood is to ward off decay from insects and moisture. Wood with a lower retention level has a lower amount of copper and, therefore, a lower cost.

In order to get to the required retention level, some species of lumber (such as Douglas fir, hem-fir, and spruce-pine-fir) have to be incised, which allows the preservative to penetrate the wood more deeply and uniformly. Tests conducted by Forest Product Laboratory have found that this practice results in a reduction in bending strength and stiffness. For this reason, incising is more common with timbers and more substantial boards.

ACQ and CA preservatives

Most of the preservatives used for treating wood intended for residential applications fall into two categories. In the first category are alkaline copper quaternary (ACQ) and two formulations of copper azole (CA-B and CA-C). The American Wood Protection Association (AWPA) has established minimum retention levels for wood treated with these preservatives (see chart at left). The label of a board treated with ACQ or CA lists the retention level.

MCQ and MCA preservatives

The second category of preservatives includes wood treated with two variations of ACQ and CA: micronized copper quaternary

AWPA MINIMUM RETENTION LEVELS (IN LB. PER CU. FT.)			
Preservative	Above ground	Ground contact	Ground contact, heavy duty
ACQ	0.15	0.40	0.60
CA-B	0.10	0.21	0.31
CA-C	0.06	0.15	0.31

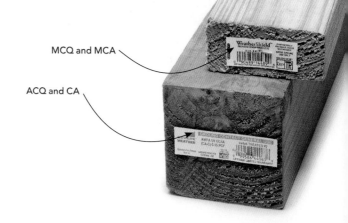

MCQ and MCA

ACQ and CA

(MCQ) and micronized copper azole (MCA). Unlike with ACQ and CA, in which the copper is dissolved chemically in an organic solvent, the copper in MCQ and MCA is present in microscopic particles suspended in water. Significantly, this makes the copper less corrosive to fasteners and hardware than the copper in wood treated with ACQ and CA; moreover, it can be placed in contact with aluminum. Another advantage is that wood treated with MCQ and MCA keeps more of its natural color.

MCA- and MCQ-treated wood has not been tested by the AWPA. Instead, manufacturers have sent their products to the International Code Council Evaluation Service (ICC-ES), which provides research reports on innovative building products that it deems equivalent to standardized products. For each product, the ICC-ES report provides a minimum retention level. The labels for these products, however, usually just state "above ground," "ground contact," or "ground contact/freshwater use," which correspond to progressively higher retention levels.

Use the right fasteners and hardware

It's important to know retention levels not only because you don't want to pay for lumber rated for ground contact if you're installing a mudsill or framing a raised deck, but also because the copper content of these preservatives should guide your choice of fasteners and hardware. Copper is corrosive, so this choice is crucial. Generally, fasteners and hardware made from stainless steel and hot-dipped-galvanized (HDG) steel are recommended for pressure-treated lumber. However, lumber with the highest retention levels—such as that used in coastal and below-grade applications—should be used with stainless steel only, which is more resistant to corrosion than HDG steel. And of course, if you're using fasteners made of stainless steel, you must use stainless-steel hardware; combining stainless-steel fasteners with HDG hardware (and vice versa) will result in faster corrosion of the galvanized parts.

IS IT GREEN, OR ISN'T IT?

IN 2002, CHEMICAL SPECIALTIES received a Presidential Green Chemistry Challenge Award from the EPA for its development of ACQ. A summary on the EPA's website says, "Replacing CCA with ACQ is one of the most dramatic pollution prevention advancements in recent history."

Pressure-treated wood has sometimes had a difficult time being considered an environmentally friendly product, however. This perception persists despite the fact that by extending the life of the wood, the same chemicals that are cause for concern mean that fewer trees have to be cut down.

Wood treated with MCQ and MCA has added a new element of confusion. Some of these products have received recognition from third-party environmental certifiers. For example, Australia-based EcoSpecifier has identified Wolmanized lumber as a Verified Product, and the MicroPro treatment has been certified as an Environmentally Preferable Product by Scientific Certification Systems. At the same time, there are concerns about the presence of nanoparticles of copper—that is, particles that are 1 to 100 nanometers in at least one dimension—in these formulations. (A nanometer is a billionth of a meter.) Materials that small have different properties, and the potential toxicity of nanoparticles of copper has not been established. The EPA's website includes this statement: "EPA is working with the Consumer Product Safety Commission to evaluate if there are any potential human and environmental effects from exposure to micronized copper."

The greenest preservatives used in residential construction may well be two newer formulations that include no copper or any other metal: EL2 (sold in Ecolife-branded lumber) and PTI (sold in lumber branded as Wolmanized EraWood and Wolmanized L3 Outdoor Wood). Because these preservatives are nonmetallic, there is no danger of any metal leaching out over time, and corrosion of fasteners and hardware is less likely. The AWPA has established minimum retention levels for EL2 and PTI, but only for above-ground use, so wood treated with these chemicals is limited to places where it won't be in prolonged contact with water.

Wooden Scaffold Planks: Solid-Sawn vs. LVL

BY DON BURGARD

In 2013, scaffolding was no. 3 on OSHA's list of most frequently cited violations, and for good reason. A 2009 survey by the Bureau of Labor Statistics found that 54 workers died in falls from scaffolding. OSHA estimates that 4,500 injuries could be prevented every year by following its regulations on scaffolding and by training all workers in safe practices. Having well-built, sturdy scaffolding won't matter, however, if the board you're standing on isn't meant to support the load you're putting on it.

Several options exist for wooden scaffold planks, but construction-grade lumber isn't one of them. No matter how sturdy those extra 2x10s might appear, don't be tempted to use them on scaffolding. Construction-grade boards are rated for their capacity to handle building loads, not the loads created by workers and their equipment.

If you work on scaffolding, be sure to inspect planks regularly for damage that could compromise their strength. Splits, sawkerfs, mold and mildew, insect damage, and delamination (in the case of LVLs) are examples of conditions that could render a plank unsafe to use. Many of these problems can be prevented with proper care, but if a plank's condition makes you question its strength, discard it.

Solid-sawn planks

The most common wood used for solid-sawn scaffold planks is southern yellow pine, which the Southern Pine Inspection Bureau grades as DI-65 or, less commonly, DI-72. DI stands for "dense industrial"—in contrast to construction-grade boards, which are graded "structural" or "dense structural" —and the number represents a strength ratio in

which the higher the number, the smaller the knots and the straighter the grain.

Planks also can be made from Douglas fir and similar species, and these have their own grading nomenclature. For example, the West Coast Lumber Inspection Bureau grades scaffold planks, in descending order of strength, as "dense premium," "premium," "dense structural," and "select structural." No matter the species, scaffold planks should be labeled as such and clearly distinguished from construction-grade boards. Though OSHA does not require it, scaffold-grade boards from reputable manufacturers also should carry a stamp that includes the grade, the moisture content (no more than 19%), the lumber-mill name and/or number, and the seal of an approved third-party inspection agency.

Manufacturers often take steps to extend the life of their planks: They seal the end grain against moisture, they insert rods through the ends of planks to prevent cupping and to keep them from splitting along their length, and they clip the corners (photo below left). This last step helps to prevent splitting if a plank is dropped on a corner.

Solid-sawn planks are available in lengths from 8 ft. to 16 ft. The longer the span between supports, the less weight the board can safely handle. For example, to handle three workers (250 lb. each, including tools) who are spaced evenly apart, the maximum span is just 5 ft.

LVL planks

These engineered boards (photo below), made from thin layers of veneer held together with an exterior-grade adhesive, minimize cupping and the effect of imperfections such as knots. The result is a somewhat stronger board that, for example, can accommodate a three-worker load on a 6-ft. span. LVL planks are available in the same sizes as solid-sawn boards and at a slightly higher cost. Most companies seal the ends against moisture, and some offer boards with an abraded surface for better traction. They don't insert rods in the ends, and they don't clip the corners, however, because an LVL plank dropped on its corner is far less likely than a solid-sawn plank to develop a severe split.

General Framing

10 Golden Rules of Framing

BY ANDY ENGEL

I've been a reader of *Fine Homebuilding* since the first issue came out in 1981, about the time I started being paid to bang nails into lumber. As it has for many other builders, the magazine served as the textbook that taught me the trade I love. Becoming an editor here and getting to know the building heroes whose bylines I'd been reading was both humbling and inspiring. It was humbling because I found them to be even more knowledgeable and talented than they seemed in print, often leaving me feeling like the village idiot. But it was inspiring because none of them were the kind of people who'd point out your ignorance. Instead, they'd invite you to grab a cold beer and a seat on a tailgate with them at the end of a hot day while they explained everything they knew that you didn't. From that deep well of building knowledge, *FHB* editor Justin Fink and I worked with the current crop of editors to winnow ten bits of framing advice we all wish we'd known the first (and last) time we strapped on our tool bags.

1 START SOLID.

Foundations are rarely perfect, so it's on the framer to ensure the mudsills are an accurate template for everything that follows. Make sure they're square and that they and the beams carrying the first floor are level and at the right height. Spending time where the wood meets the concrete makes the rest of the job go faster.

2 LAY OUT WALLS ALONE.

You may want help snapping lines, but otherwise, transferring wall locations from prints to floor requires solo concentration. Any mistake can mean hours of rework. Do whatever it takes to work on this step without distractions—get to the job before anyone else, send the crew to lunch or set them to sorting lumber, and turn off your phone.

3 KEEP YOUR FEET ON THE GROUND.

If you do a good job following rules 1 and 2, it becomes possible to accurately mark beams and plates—and even to install hardware—for joists, trusses, or rafters before raising them into place. Working on sawhorses, the lumber pile, or the deck are all faster than working on a ladder.

4 WASTE NOTHING.

Every pallet of incoming lumber should be culled and the straightest pieces set aside for the places where straightness matters most (top plates, king and jack studs, etc.). Crooked, bowed, wavey, and knotty lumber has its place too. These defects matter very little when the piece is being cut short for cripples, blocking, or temporary supports.

5 AVOID GUESSWORK.

There's more to laying out framing than marking Xs for each stud position. Mark every wall component—kings, jacks, cripples, intersections, point-load posts, and blocking—to ensure you won't have to waste time later fixing inaccuracies. For complicated assemblies such as rafters or stringers, do a full-scale layout to avoid mistakes.

6 ONLY MEASURE WHEN YOU NEED TO.

Tape measures are indispensable, but they can also introduce errors. Whenever possible, mark pieces in position rather than measuring them, and cut wall and roof sheathing in place during or after installation to improve accuracy.

7 EFFICIENCY IS KING.

Framing involves repetitive tasks, such as cutting dozens of pieces to the exact same length. Learn to take advantage of situations when it's easy and convenient to cut several pieces to length in one pass, often before the wood even leaves the lumber pallet it arrived on.

8 WORK SMART.

"Wet" and "heavy" are common themes when working with framing lumber. Avoid the temptation to be a hero by carrying 10 studs or two sheets of sheathing at once. In the long run, your body will lose the battle. If you don't have diesel-powered machines to help with lifting, at least work smart by tackling heavy lifts with wall jacks or in teams of two or more.

9 PLUMB AND LEVEL AREN'T ENOUGH.

Every wall that is tipped into place should be rigged up with a string that runs from one end to the other so it can be pushed and/or pulled straight along its length. Although the method is different, joists, rafters, and beams must also be kept straight to ease the installation of the next pieces.

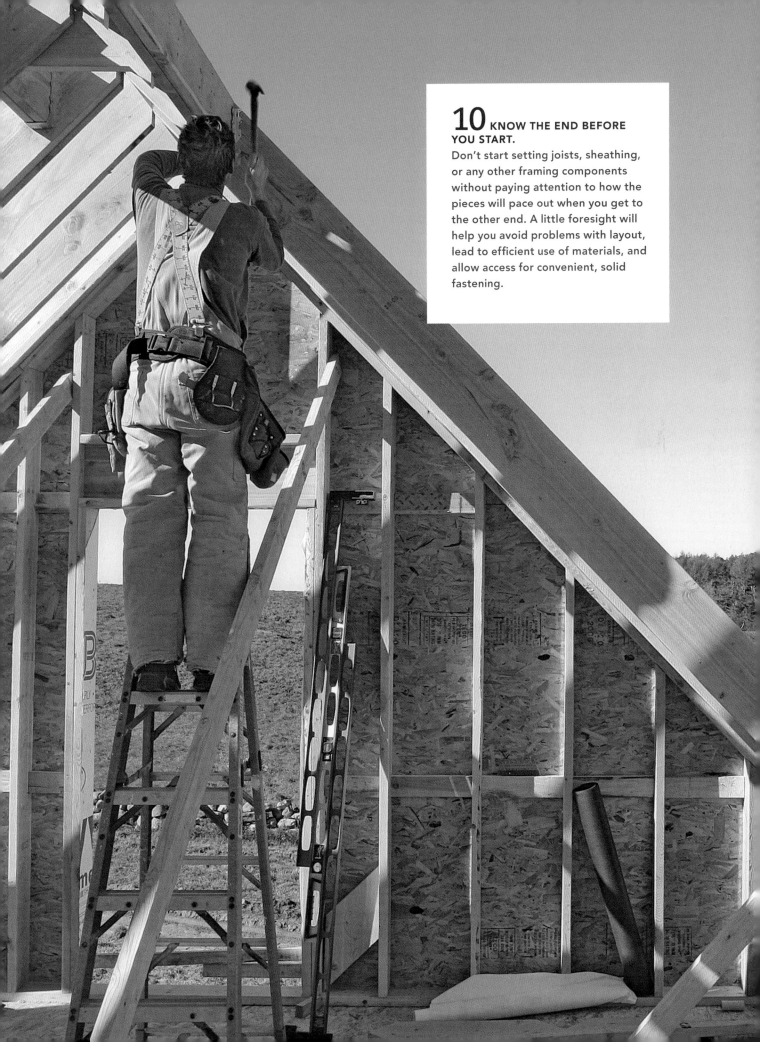

10 KNOW THE END BEFORE YOU START.

Don't start setting joists, sheathing, or any other framing components without paying attention to how the pieces will pace out when you get to the other end. A little foresight will help you avoid problems with layout, lead to efficient use of materials, and allow access for convenient, solid fastening.

The Next 10 Rules

BY JOHN SPIER

Now that you've mastered the ten basic golden rules of framing a house (see pp. 33–39), you can move on to the refinements that will make you good at it. Contrary to popular opinion, the best framers aren't finish guys slumming with circular saws or young stud muffins bursting with strength and testosterone. The best people to frame houses are those with backgrounds in both production and custom work, who have also built from foundation to finish. They understand that the frame is an integral part of a complex system. Here are just some of the many things they know; we could call them rules 11–20.

11 EVERYTHING IS EXACTLY AS GOOD AS IT NEEDS TO BE.

I know some carpenters whose framing looks like finish work; they'll draw a grid on their sheathing for a nailing pattern and take a belt sander to rafter intersections. That's fine when framing your own house, or if you have a client who wants that sort of work and understands what they're paying for. But most framing jobs are for people who will be paying a mortgage for the next few decades. They shouldn't have the added expense of paying for your ego trip, too.

TEN MORE. In response to our "10 Golden Rules of Framing" (see. pp. 33–39), frequent *Fine Homebuilding* contributor John Spier added 10 more rules of his own. Here, he is shown framing a garage-door opening.

12 UNDERSTAND TOLERANCES.

Aim for perfection when starting at the sills, but accept that you won't maintain that to the ridge. If an upper floor or dormer isn't as perfect as the first floor, or if a ridge has a little bend under the caps, no one will ever know. Just know what's critical: Don't lose that quarter inch in a stairway, bathroom, or kitchen.

GANG-CUTTING. The author finds that I-joists are ideally suited for time-saving gang-cutting.

13 HONOR THE IMPORTANCE OF SYMMETRY.

Someone once said that symmetry is the hobgoblin of little minds, but it's the builder's best friend. Identical things should be identical: If there's a row of dormers, make them the same size; if there's a bank of windows, the spaces between them should match. And anytime you can mass-produce components, you've also saved time and material.

14 ESTABLISH A COMMON LAYOUT FOR THE BUILDING, AND STICK TO IT.

Rafters, studs, and joists should all be aligned over and under each other in both directions. It looks better, it's straighter and stronger, it's easier to finish, and it's courteous to the subtrades. A plumber who is drilling a hole down in a wall bay on an upper floor should be confident that they're going to hit a matching bay below.

15 PUT YOUR NAILERS IN AS YOU GO.

It's faster and more efficient than adding them later, and in many cases, much easier to nail blocking securely.

16 BE CONSIDERATE OF OTHER TRADES.

Have a good understanding of subtrades and finish work, and frame with them in mind. Leave room for shower valves, lay out studs for closet cleats

and brackets, don't skip studs and cripples that maintain the layout, and include nailers for critical components. As you put things together, try to keep nail-free areas where people will need to drill, like between 1 ft. and 2 ft. from the floor, and in double top plates above stud bays. If you've never built an entire house, you probably shouldn't be framing one.

17 KEEP YOUR STOCK AND YOUR SCRAP ORGANIZED.

Spend a few minutes at the end of every day putting all of your cutoffs into consolidated piles, so when you need a handful of pieces, you won't be cutting them out of long stock or scrounging around the job site. The less we put in the dumpster, the better for all of us.

18 DON'T USE A BUNCH OF EXTRA MATERIAL WHERE YOU DON'T NEED TO.

A massive header in a nonbearing wall with no load on it, supported by multiple jack studs and cripples, is just a waste of time, resources, and energy. Same goes for double sills, extra cripples, four-stud corners, partition posts, and other relics of an earlier age. It's pretty easy to get an R-21 wall down to R-12 if you put enough lumber in it.

19 DON'T WASTE MOVES, AND DON'T BEND OVER IF YOU DON'T HAVE TO.

If you need a bunch of blocks, line up a bunch of shorts and take out your tape, pencil, and square one time only. If you need to get four pieces out of one, chop it in half first and then measure all four at once. If you need angles or bevels, cut half of them at a time instead of switching the saw back and forth. If you can reach across and catch the piece you need as you cut it, you don't need to pick it up off the ground. Efficiency and production building aren't about busting your ass all day long; they're about thinking ahead, making every move count, and incorporating a hundred little tricks for not wasting time and energy.

20 KEEP THE JOB CLEAN.

A clean site is safer, easier, and more efficient. If you give your subs a clean, organized place to work, they'll be more likely to keep it that way. And it'll do your reputation a world of good; word of mouth is your best advertising, and people speak well of job sites that are neat and attractive.

Simple Wood Beams

BY R. BRUCE HOADLEY

Beams, defined as elongated members that are loaded perpendicular to their long axis, are critical to the structure of a house. The classic example of a double or triple 2x beam supporting floor joists usually comes to mind, but joists, roof rafters, headers over windows and doors, and stair stringers are all examples of beams.

Today, builders often rely on engineered structural lumber—LVLs, PSLs, I-joists, and others—but dimensional lumber is still used widely as well. In practice, builders have no say over the strength of the wood itself; we are simply charged with using the inherent strength effectively.

If you know the limit of acceptable deflection and how much weight a beam needs to carry—both of

which are provided by building codes—then the type, species, grade, length, width, and depth of the beam all can be selected.

Although engineers are invaluable for their knowledge of the calculations used to specify beams of all sorts—including more complicated setups such as continuous, fixed-end, and cantilever beams—anyone can apply the principles of beam mechanics generally, without getting into precise calculations, to improve the mechanical performance of countless parts of a house. The decision of where to place a support column or partition wall, when to choose double 2x8s as opposed to a single 2x10, and the

A SIMPLY SUPPORTED BEAM

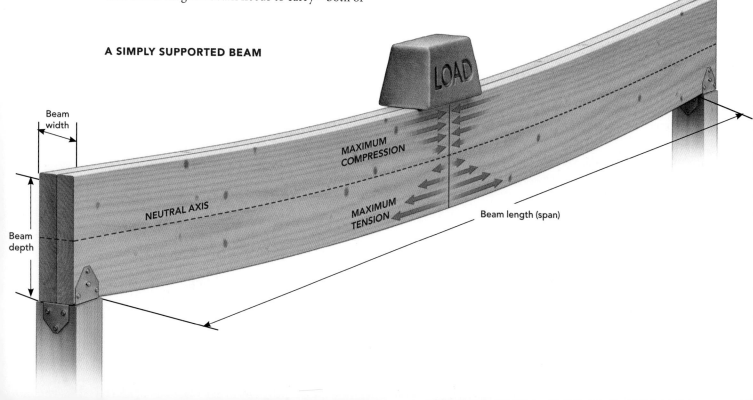

Beam width

Beam depth

LOAD

MAXIMUM COMPRESSION

NEUTRAL AXIS

MAXIMUM TENSION

Beam length (span)

most effective method for stiffening an undersize joist can benefit from a basic understanding of the relationship between a beam's carrying capacity and its stiffness. Here's how it works.

The fundamentals

Let's consider a center-loaded dimensional-lumber beam that's bearing on two fixed points and spanning the space between without the help of intermediate support. This setup is called a simply supported beam and is the most basic example.

The weight from the load above causes the beam to bend, creating compression on the upper surface and tension along the bottom (photo facing page). Both stresses reach their maximum at the very top and bottom of the beam and then diminish to zero at the central horizontal plane, called the neutral axis. The stresses are also greatest at midspan and decrease to zero at each end of the beam where it's supported.

Know your beam options

Builders face two primary considerations when choosing a beam: first, how much it can carry and what factors influence its carrying capacity; second, how much it will deflect and what factors influence its deflection.

The grade and species of a beam have an effect in this regard. For example, a wood species that is twice as strong can carry twice as much weight, and a species with twice the bending tolerance—known as modulus of elasticity—will deflect half as much. However, this information is useful only if you have lots of wood species to choose from. Framing lumber is typically offered in just a few species, so the more useful information is likely to be how changes to the length, width, and depth of a beam will affect its carrying capacity and deflection. These changes are either direct (increase X, and Y increases), or inverse (increase X, and Y decreases).

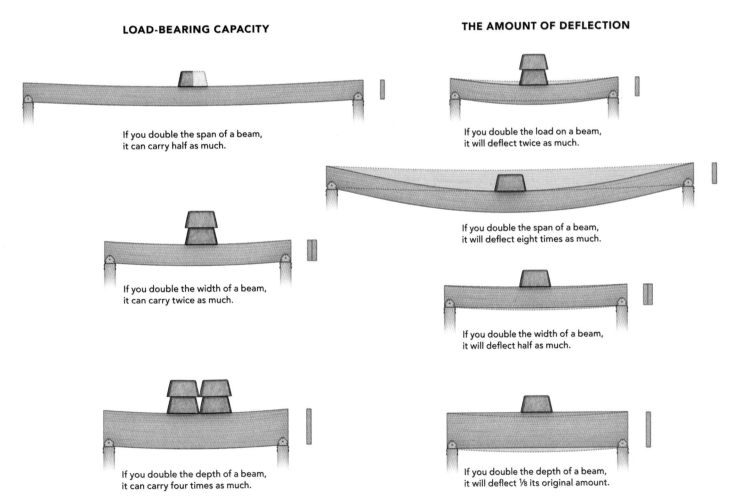

LOAD-BEARING CAPACITY

If you double the span of a beam, it can carry half as much.

If you double the width of a beam, it can carry twice as much.

If you double the depth of a beam, it can carry four times as much.

THE AMOUNT OF DEFLECTION

If you double the load on a beam, it will deflect twice as much.

If you double the span of a beam, it will deflect eight times as much.

If you double the width of a beam, it will deflect half as much.

If you double the depth of a beam, it will deflect ⅛ its original amount.

Cutting an Acute Bevel

BY ANDY ENGEL

Standard circular saws and miter saws can cut bevel angles up to about 54°. While that handles most day-to-day needs, every so often you need to make a cheek cut that a standard saw can't accommodate. For example, I recently found myself having to cut a 71° bevel on a piece of 2x6 blocking for a set of winding stairs.

The technique is simply to cut the angle on each edge of the board using a circular saw and then to connect the cuts using a reciprocating saw or a handsaw. In fact, you could make the entire cut with either of those tools, but it's hard to cut accurately with a recip saw, and using a handsaw is tedious.

Working with square-edged lumber is crucial. If the edge isn't square to the face, your cuts won't align. Careful layout also is important, because the accuracy of the second layout line depends on aligning it with the first. Likewise, the third line's accuracy depends on how it intersects the second line. Errors can accumulate rapidly.

1 START WITH SQUARE-EDGED STOCK. Framing lumber may be manufactured with square edges, but changes in moisture content can alter its geometry. Pick through the lumber pile to locate a piece with square edges.

2 MARK ONE EDGE. Use a T-bevel, protractor, or framing square to lay out the angle on the lumber.

3 COMPENSATE FOR THE ROUNDOVER. The eased edges on lumber make it harder to accurately transfer the cutline from the edge to the face. Sight directly down on the T-bevel and the face of the lumber, and mark the intersection of the two.

4 DRAW A SQUARE LINE ON THE FACE. This line determines where you mark the angle on the second edge, and it provides a reference when cutting.

5 MARK THE ANGLE ON THE SECOND EDGE. To again compensate for the roundover, sight down on the T-bevel to align it with the square line on the lumber face, then mark the second cutline.

6 SET UP A CIRCULAR SAW. Use a sharp, thin-kerf blade. Don't trust the bevel settings on the saw; they're rarely accurate. Instead, use a square to ensure that the blade is at 90° relative to the saw's base.

7 MAKE THE FIRST CUT. Clamp the stock in place. Set the saw's base firmly on the lumber edge, and don't rock the saw as you cut. As it exits the cut, the blade should follow the square line on the lumber.

8 FLIP THE BOARD OVER. Repeat the cut from the opposite edge.

9 FINISH THE CUT. A reciprocating saw makes quick work of the job, but a handsaw isn't much slower. The reason for the thin-kerf blade in the circular saw is to match more closely the kerf width of either a recip saw or a handsaw.

ANGLE-MARKING TOOLS

FRAMING SQUARE
An old-school tool for laying out angles, a framing square provides angles in rafter-pitch increments, such as 12-in-12, rather than degrees. One shortcoming is that it's hard to use this tool to measure some angles, especially if the pieces being measured are short.

RAFTER SQUARE
Most carpenters have a rafter square at hand, often in their tool belt. While they provide rafter-pitch increments like a framing square, rafter squares also measure in degrees.

T-BEVEL
The simplest method of transferring angles, a T-bevel is simply held in place to duplicate an angle, and then its locking screw is tightened down. It provides no measurement increments, but transfers angles directly.

ANGLE FINDER
A bit of a specialty tool, this protractor can be used to measure angles in degrees like a rafter square and to transfer angles directly like a T-bevel.

Wind-Resistant Framing Techniques

BY BRYAN READLING

You've seen photos and videos of massive tornadoes ripping through towns and wiping neighborhoods off the map. Given the destruction, you might guess that any house close to an advancing tornado is doomed. The reality, though, is that weaker twisters—those rated EF-0, EF-1, and EF-2 by the National Weather Service—make up 95% of all tornadoes. A carefully constructed house often can survive a hit from one of these smaller, more common storms.

As an engineer for APA-The Engineered Wood Association, I spend a lot of my time studying wind damage to houses and figuring out ways to boost a house's resistance to hurricanes, tornadoes, and

SEEING STORM DAMAGE FIRSTHAND. Following an outbreak of deadly tornadoes in the spring of 2011, the author surveyed hundreds of storm-damaged homes in a multistate investigation. His research revealed that many of the most-badly damaged homes could have fared much better had their builders adopted a few simple and inexpensive wind-resistant framing methods.

MISSING ANCHOR BOLTS. This house, which was attached to its masonry foundation with cut nails, was pushed 6 ft. off its foundation by tornado-driven wind. Similar failures occurred with houses that were nailed to slab foundations.

windstorms. My work includes plenty of travel, because tornadoes and hurricanes affect most of the country and high-wind events happen everywhere.

My latest field-research project was in April 2011, when two storms two weeks apart spawned tornadoes in seven Southern states. The second storm caused the single largest tornado outbreak in recorded history. In our subsequent investigation of wind-damaged houses 10 years old and newer, my colleagues and I discovered that most of the structural failures were caused by a lack of continuity in the load path that connects a house's structural elements from the foundation to the roof.

Roof failures

The most common and often most devastating load-path failures occurred when rafters and trusses were pulled from exterior walls. Many of the most severely damaged houses had roof framing attached to the walls with toenails, an inherently weak connection because it relies on the nails' withdrawal capacity. Modern building codes allow toenailed rafters in

UNBACKED FOAM SHEATHING. Foam sheathing performs better when the interior is covered with drywall. Gable ends without drywall, like the gables on these neighboring homes, should be sheathed with structural panels.

most nonhurricane areas, but many engineers don't believe toenails have the strength to meet some International Residential Code requirements.

Roof failures were not limited to houses with toenailed trusses and rafters. Failures also occurred when metal hurricane ties were nailed on the interior of the top plate instead of the exterior. Exterior-mounted metal connectors hold better because they line up with the wall sheathing's load path.

Wall failures

Another common observation, especially in the hardest-hit areas, was houses blown off their foundations. Most had their walls attached to the foundation with hand-driven, cut masonry nails and, in a few locations, pneumatic framing nails. Obviously, anchor bolts are a better choice, especially when the bolts have large square washers to prevent them from pulling through the plate.

A gable end is often poorly connected to the rest of the building. We saw many houses where the

MISSING ROOF CONNECTORS. Unless it's adequately secured, roof framing can be pulled from the walls that it's attached to during high winds. Toenailed roof framing ripped from walls was the most commonly observed serious building failure in the author's post-storm research.

triangle-shaped gable end had blown in, often leading to greater damage from wind and water. The gable end is especially vulnerable to failure because its walls are often not backed with drywall. Walls backed with drywall in living space generally hold up better because the drywall provides additional resistance to wind and debris. Failures like this were even more common when the gables were covered with foam sheathing and vinyl siding because both materials are vulnerable to wind pressure and flying debris.

Poorly fastened sheathing

When the houses we studied were at least partially intact, the loss of wood wall and roof sheathing often could be attributed to improper attachment. Nails used as prescribed in the building codes provided good performance, while staples performed poorly because they offer less pullout resistance than nails and must be used in greater quantity. Poorly attached roof sheathing at the last rafter or gable-end truss was identified as a weak link in roof construction.

CONNECTORS ON THE WRONG SIDE. This house's roof framing was attached to the walls' top plate with metal hurricane ties. Unfortunately, the ties were fastened on the inside of the top plate, where they aren't as strong as connectors aligned with the wall sheathing on the exterior.

We also saw many cases where breaches in the exterior walls due to wind pressure or flying debris caused pressurization of the building, sometimes resulting in homes that blew apart completely. Field and wind-tunnel research has revealed that wind and flying-debris damage to doors, windows, and nonstructural claddings like brick and vinyl siding often leads to more catastrophic structural failures. Large openings such as garage doors are especially vulnerable to impact and wind-pressure damage.

A small price to pay

Most of these above-code improvements are easy to implement and surprisingly affordable. In researching the 2013 Georgia Disaster Resilient Building Code, the Georgia Department of Community Affairs determined that the added cost of implementing the APA's recommendations is about $595. This estimate, which includes materials and labor, is based on a 2,100-sq.-ft. slab-on-grade ranch house with a 10-in-12 roof pitch and three gables.

BEYOND CODE FOR HIGH-WIND RESISTANCE

THE FRAMING DETAILS SHOWN HERE ARE NOT COMPLICATED or expensive to execute when they are incorporated into the plans for a new house. In addition to these measures, there are other ways to protect houses in hurricane and tornado-prone areas.

First, protect large openings. Picture windows, sliding-glass doors, garage doors, and other large openings are vulnerable to damage in high-wind events. Breaches can lead to pressurization of the building interior and increased loads on the structure. Consider installing windows, doors, and garage doors rated for high winds and impact damage.

While a stronger, more wind-resistant structure is certainly safer for occupants, think about adding a safe room in a basement or central space.

Finally, consider using hip roofs, which are more aerodynamic and provide better support to the tops of exterior walls than gable roofs.

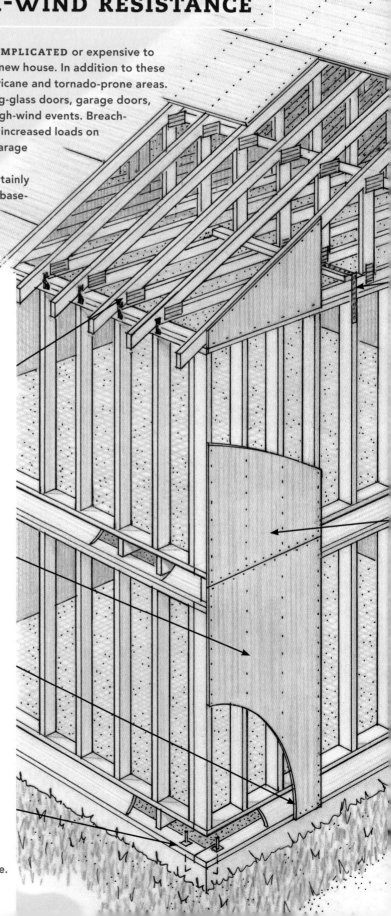

TIE DOWN RAFTERS
Secure rafters and trusses with metal connectors. The roof-to-wall connection is subject to both uplift and shear. Inexpensive framing connectors make this important connection simple. Place connectors on the outside of the wall, where they'll do the most good.

USE ENOUGH NAILS
Nail wall sheathing with 8d common (0.131 in. by 2½ in.) nails 4 in. on center at ends and edges and 6 in. on center in the intermediate framing. This installation will greatly increase wind and racking resistance compared to code-minimum requirements.

LAP THE SILL
Extend wood structural-panel sheathing to the sill plate. The connection of the wall sheathing to a properly anchored sill plate is an important part of the load path. Available at many pro-oriented lumberyards, 9-ft.-long and 10-ft.-long OSB simplifies this connection.

BOLT SILL PLATES
Anchor sill plates with ½-in. anchor bolts equipped with 0.229-in.-thick, 3-in. by 3-in. square plate washers. Space the bolts from 32 in. to 48 in. on center. The IRC requires a minimum spacing of 6 ft. for houses subjected to wind speeds up to 110 mph, but tighter spacing greatly improves wall performance.

RING-SHANK NAILS ON ROOF
Nail roof sheathing with 8d ring-shank or deformed-shank (0.131 in. by 2½ in.) nails at 4 in. on center along eaves and panel ends and 6 in. on center at intermediate framing.

SHEATHE GABLES
Sheathe gable ends with plywood or OSB. Foam sheathing works better when used with drywall inside the house. The easiest way to avoid interior gypsum at the gable end is to use wood sheathing on the exterior.

TIE GABLES TO WALLS
Tie gable-end walls back to the structure. Gable ends should be tied to the wall framing below with metal straps and by lapping the gable sheathing onto the wall below.

CONNECT LEVELS
Break upper-story and lower-story sheathing at the band joist or engineered rim to provide lateral and uplift load continuity. Continuous sheathing also provides an additional layer of protection if siding or brick veneer is lost during storms.

PROTECT OPENINGS
Strengthened with steel struts and upgraded hardware, garage doors should be rated for the maximum wind speeds specified in the IRC's building-planning section. Dealers and manufacturers can offer guidance on choosing a garage door appropriate for local conditions.

Upgraded rollers

Stronger track

Reinforcing steel

High Winds vs. Houses

BY DEBRA JUDGE SILBER

What happens when a powerful windstorm slams into an average house? The devastation resulting from a tornado or strong hurricane might hint at a foregone conclusion: Goodbye, house. But by studying the precise effects of extreme winds on structures and the pattern of failures that result, researchers have made real progress in understanding how to make homes safer and more damage-resistant. (For more on helping houses weather the storm, see "Wind-Resistant Framing Techniques," pp. 47–53.)

High winds, whether from a hurricane or a tornado, affect structures in similar ways. Tornadoes can be stronger, but hurricane winds last longer and are accompanied by damaging rain. Both create significant uplift forces on roofs.

Although variables abound even when comparing wood-frame homes (the home's size and style, the type of storm and its strength, the storm's path and duration), research has revealed several common points of failure. It is in these areas that wind and flying debris combine to undermine a home's structure, turning a weather event into a catastrophe. It is also where adequate reinforcement can make a real difference in what remains after the clouds recede. Here's how it works.

WINDOWS
Wind entering through broken windows creates interior pressure that can blow out roofs and walls. **PREVENTION:** Protect openings from impact.

GABLES
Uplift forces lift roof sheathing, enabling wind to push the gable in on the windward side and pull it out on the leeward side. Similar failures occur between stories where top plates are not well secured. **PREVENTION:** Attach roof sheathing firmly to framing at gable ends; tie gable-end walls back to structure. Reinforce wall-rim connections.

TORNADOES	
EF scale	Wind speed (mph)*
0	65-85
1	86-110
2	111-135
3	136-165
4	166-200
5	200+

*Estimated speed of three-second gust. EF tornado scales are based on observed damage, not measured wind speeds.

DAMAGE CONTROL VS. SAFETY
A continuous load path in which all structural parts are tied together to resist wind loads is the best insurance against structural damage from hurricanes and weaker tornadoes (70% of tornadoes have wind speeds of 110 mph or less, the equivalent of a Cat 2 hurricane). To ensure personal safety in stronger tornadoes, however, experts agree that the only answer is a reinforced safe room or underground shelter.

CORNERS
Suction resulting from variations in air pressure pulls corners apart.
PREVENTION: Reinforce with metal connectors.

WALL-TO-FOUNDATION CONNECTION
With inadequate anchoring, wind can force the sill plate off the foundation, resulting in collapse.
PREVENTION: Extend wood sheathing to sill plate; bolt sill plate to foundation.

GARAGE DOORS
Frontal wind pressure can cause weak doors to buckle, allowing wind to pressurize the building envelope.
PREVENTION: Invest in wind-resistant doors with reinforced hardware.

ROOF-TO-WALL CONNECTION
Uplift under the eaves combined with negative pressure above the roof and internal pressure within (once the envelope is breached) undermines the roof-to-wall connection.
PREVENTION: Secure rafters/trusses to walls with metal connectors.

HURRICANES	
Saffir-Simpson wind scale	Wind speed**
Cat 1	74-95
Cat 2	96-110
Cat 3	111-129
Cat 4	130-156
Cat 5	157+

**Sustained measured wind speed

Framing by Computer Model

BY MICHAEL PATTERSON

Make it look like the pretty picture. That's our job as carpenters—to bring someone's ideas to life in three dimensions. Sometimes, though, the carpenter and the customer have different visions, and details get lost in the translation. Avoiding that issue is one reason we have drawings.

There's another reason as well. Good drawings help me to complete the work quickly. A recent project where I built a portico on top of an existing concrete-and-brick stoop provides a good example of how drawings speed my work. Efficiency starts with thinking the details through beforehand. That sounds pretty obvious, if only because every job needs a materials list, a plan for how to proceed, and a time estimate. But in cases such as this small portico, I expand the concept. In the past, I would have estimated the rough dimensions of the parts and pieces to order the material. Once on site, I'd have figured out the exact dimensions of the framing, cutting the pieces to size just before installing them. Next, I'd have measured the installed framing to determine the sizes of the trim pieces, spending a lot of time running up and down a ladder. Complicating matters would be doing all that outside.

A few years ago, I started tackling smaller projects by first developing a detailed drawing and a cutlist with the exact dimensions of nearly every piece in the project. From that detailed list, I cut as much of the project as possible in my shop, right down to the trim. I usually still have to cut a piece or two on-site when existing conditions vary enough to make precutting dicey. Even on those pieces, though, I still do as much dimensioning or shaping as possible in the shop.

The advantages are obvious. The cutting is done with shop tools, which tend to be more accurate than job-site tools. Much of the work is done out of the elements, and because the on-site time is minimized, there is less disruption to the client's life. My shop is at my home, so I have no commute, which is nothing to sneeze at in the traffic-clogged Washington, D.C., area. I also find that I can complete the job more quickly, in part because my trips up the ladder are only to install the components, not to measure for them.

THE JOB. It was clear that the existing facade, while nice enough, would benefit both visually and functionally from an entry portico.

SKETCHUP AS A TOOL. A computer model of the architect's plan was superimposed over a photo to show the homeowner what the final portico would look like.

PRECUT AND ASSEMBLED. Most components were cut, and some were assembled, in the author's shop. Site time was reduced, benefiting both carpenter and client.

THE PERFECT FIT. The completed portico deviates from the computer model only in the railing and the door treatment, the result of decisions made later in the process.

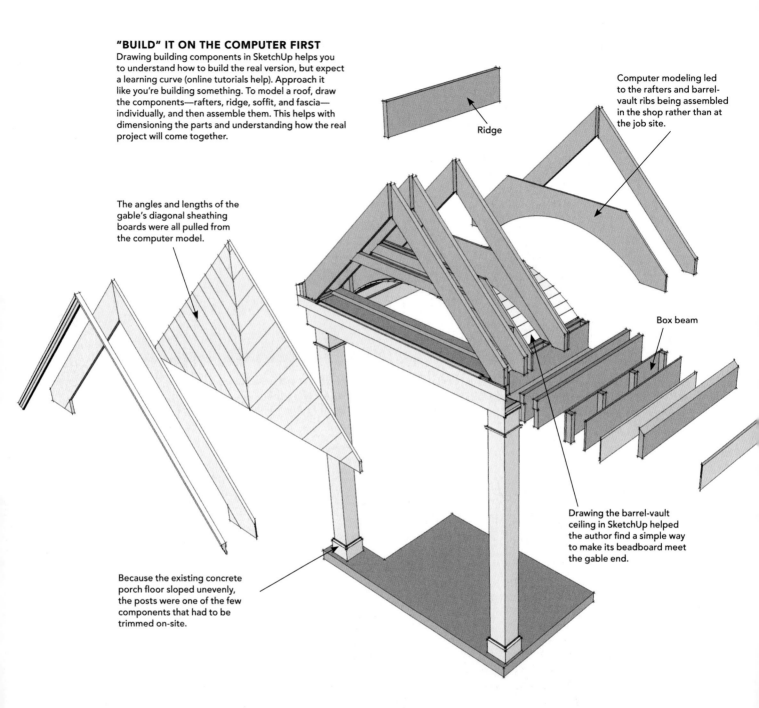

"BUILD" IT ON THE COMPUTER FIRST
Drawing building components in SketchUp helps you to understand how to build the real version, but expect a learning curve (online tutorials help). Approach it like you're building something. To model a roof, draw the components—rafters, ridge, soffit, and fascia—individually, and then assemble them. This helps with dimensioning the parts and understanding how the real project will come together.

The angles and lengths of the gable's diagonal sheathing boards were all pulled from the computer model.

Ridge

Computer modeling led to the rafters and barrel-vault ribs being assembled in the shop rather than at the job site.

Box beam

Drawing the barrel-vault ceiling in SketchUp helped the author find a simple way to make its beadboard meet the gable end.

Because the existing concrete porch floor sloped unevenly, the posts were one of the few components that had to be trimmed on-site.

Measure, then draw in detail

This portico was designed by Amy Stacy, an architect with whom I work regularly. Her drawings were accurate enough for me to estimate from, but to build a computer model and a cutlist with dimensions that were guaranteed to fit, I needed to quantify the site conditions exactly.

Conditions I check include not only dimensions but also such things as whether the existing construction is plumb and level. A house wall that leans out far enough could, if not accounted for, leave the new column bases overhanging the edge of the stoop. I did find that this stoop wasn't level, so the posts had to be trimmed on-site. Since the new portico roof had to tuck just beneath and run parallel to the rake board on the existing roof, I verified that the roof pitch was drawn correctly on the plans. I also checked to see if the concrete stoop was centered on the door, or if it was offset. This would affect where the columns could be located.

One aspect I didn't check came back to bite me. I assumed that the house's brick walls were structural, a common detail in this neighborhood that would mean I could cut pockets into the brick and support the insides of the roof beams on the house wall. However, they turned out to be brick veneer, which by code can't be used structurally to support a load. This meant that I had to add structural posts down the face of the wall. Because of how these posts ended up having to be spaced, I had to move a light, which led me to add the paneling around the door. This is a good reminder to make no assumptions and to check everything carefully.

You can draw the parts of the structure underlying that pretty picture a number of different ways. In the past, I often drew things out full scale on a piece of plywood using a construction calculator and a framing square. Then I discovered a free drawing program called SketchUp. While it is not as powerful as a traditional CAD program or design-specific software programs such as Chief Architect or Revit Architecture, it lets me draw on the computer like I had so often drawn on plywood.

To develop the cutlist for this portico, I began by looking at the finished dimensions on the architect's plans. Then thinking from the outside in, I built a model of the portico in SketchUp with exact board-by-board dimensions. First came the trim, whose outside dimensions sprang from the architect's plans, and then the framing members, whose size was determined by the trim's dimensions. Math doesn't lie. Assuming you have accurate measurements, if it fits together on-screen, it will fit on-site. The computer model's dimensions became my cutlist.

Working things out on screen allowed me to explore the easiest way to build certain details. For example, it became obvious that the barrel-vaulted ceiling would be easier to build if I assembled its arched ribs and straight rafters into trusses in my shop, to be set as units on-site. Another example was a fiber-cement panel on the inside gable face that had to meet the curve of the barrel vault. I wondered how I'd make that curved cut, but when doing the SketchUp drawing, I realized that instead of the difficult task of cutting the fiber-cement panel to fit the ceiling boards, I could frame the roof so that the panel dropped in from above. Then I could butt the ceiling boards to the panel—a simpler, faster, and cleaner approach. Small details like that add up to a real time savings and a better-executed project.

Make the parts like the drawing

I did everything I could in the shop, including rabbeting the back of the fascia for the soffit panels, cutting the angled gable boards, and assembling the rake returns, box beams, and roof trusses. Of course, there's a limit to the size of such assemblies. They have to be small and light enough to be placed easily.

1 BUILD IN THE SHOP. Pocket screws from the back create a hidden connection between the rake boards and the cornice returns. It's a sturdy joint that looks good and can survive transportation to the site.

2 LOAD ON THE TRUCK. All the components of the portico fit in one truckload for delivery to the site. Sitting on top are the roof trusses.

3 ASSEMBLE AT THE JOB SITE. After the posts were trimmed, erected, and braced, the lightweight box beams were lifted easily into place. Layered on top of the framing, the precut trim was nailed into place quickly and easily.

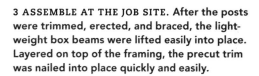

An advantage to working in the shop is that it keeps the material dry. Using dry stock is particularly important when cutting a project ahead of time, as any dimensional changes can throw the fit off. Expecting the wood to expand a little bit once it's exposed to moisture, I take the layout lines when cutting the framing. On the trim, I cut right to the lines, so it's a little bigger than the framing it will cover. I'd rather have to take a little off a piece of trim than have it be too short.

Once I was on-site for this project, the only measuring and cutting I had to do was on the two outer support posts. The post locations were not level with each other, and it was easier to account for this variance on-site. Because everything else was cut, with some of it built into assemblies in the shop, I just

had to install it. I had printouts of my drawings and cutlist, so it was easy to check and cross-check as I went along, making sure that the components went together as planned.

I spent about two hours drawing the portico in SketchUp and making the cutlist. Shop work, delivery, and installation took an additional 59 hours, for a total of 61 hours. If I'd built the portico entirely on-site, I estimate that the job would have taken around 75 hours. The savings of 14 hours is not too shabby, and it doesn't include time saved by avoiding rain delays. Plus, some of that time was spent in a comfortable shop rather than out in the cold scratching my head.

Timber-Frame Joinery

BY BILL CADLEY

The scarf joint was born of necessity when carpenters needed longer timbers than their forests could provide. The first documented example comes from the remains of a 7th-century Anglo-Saxon burial ship that was discovered in an English riverbank. A scarf was used to join stem and stern timbers to a center keel.

Dozens of scarf joints have been documented over time. Some have failed miserably, while others have survived centuries. The double-bladed scarf, first introduced in the 16th century, is the strongest joint for joining two timbers. Commonly used in a horizontal application (over a post, for instance), it also can be used vertically.

This particular timber-frame joint has long been a favorite of mine because of its decorative as well as its structural power. To make it stand out more, I increase the length of the blades from the usual 1½ in. to 5 in.

Accurate layout is critical if you don't want to spend all day fitting the four face cuts on each half of the joint. It is a time-consuming process, but my speed picks up on the second and third joints. In a completed frame, the scarf is an eloquent representation of the time spent and the level of my craft.

LAYOUT IS BASED ON A CENTERLINE

TYPICALLY 20 IN. TO 30 IN. LONG, the completed scarf consists of two identical halves. Each has a 5-in. by 1½-in. blade, a 14-in. space, and a corresponding 5-in. by 1½-in. housing. Once assembled, the joint can be pegged through the blades.

MARK THE END OF THE CUT TO REDUCE TEAROUT. The joinery is as decorative as it is structural, so it's important to have clean cuts. With that in mind, use a chisel to score the end grain at the end of the housing cut. Next, rip the centerline from both sides; the mortise will clean out anything left by the stopped cuts.

BACK-CUTTING MAKES AN EASIER FIT. After the shoulder is cut (top left), the blade end is relieved across its center (bottom left). The housing can be excavated with a drill and chisel, or it can be cut with a chain mortiser (center). The end result should be a clean, tight housing for the blade. The back end of the housing is relieved with a chisel (right), so any adjustments have to be made only to the exposed edges of the blade.

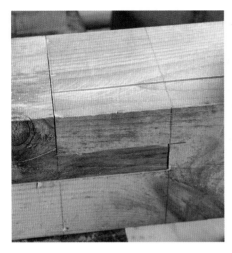

TEST AND TUNE THE FIT. With the two halves assembled, check all mating edges to see that there aren't any gaps caused by an improper fit. In this case, a gap at the blade was reduced by a sawkerf on the shoulder.

BIG TIMBERS REQUIRE BIG TOOLS

A DEVICE MADE SPECIFICALLY for timber framers is the chain mortiser, a small electric chainsaw mounted on an indexing frame. It cuts a mortise in the time it used to take a carpenter to chuck a bit into his brace. Another tool, a big circular saw, has a 16$\frac{5}{16}$-in.-dia. blade and can cut 6$\frac{1}{4}$ in. at 90°. The electric brake improves safety, and there's an extra handle mounted on the body for more control. The tools shown here are made by Makita (www.makitausa.com). The mortiser sells for about $1,300 and the saw for about $650.

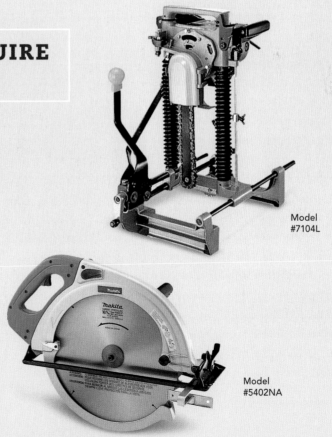

Model #7104L

Model #5402NA

The Essential Timber-Frame Joint

BY WILL BEEMER

Timber-framing is one of the oldest forms of home building still being practiced. It's part of a tradition that can be seen today in buildings constructed 800 years ago. While it's no longer the conventional form of building, many still view timber-framing as the embodiment of carpentry and the craft of home building.

At first glance, a timber frame is all about the exposed wood and the strength implied by its large scale. Look a little closer, and you'll see that the real magic lies in the joinery that unifies the wood into a structure. The joint I'll concentrate on here is the mortise and tenon, which is ubiquitous throughout furniture-making and cabinet making and is used to join one piece coming in at an angle (often 90°) to another piece. As an extension of the long grain, a tenon inserted into a mortise increases the captured surface area within a joint. In a timber frame, pegs (also known as trunnels or tree nails) secure the

LEVEL YOUR WORKSURFACE. The larger dimensions of the timbers create the potential for a higher-than-normal worksurface. Bring down the surface to a normal height by using shorter sawhorses. A 24-in. to 30-in. height is common.

FIND LEVEL. Because most timber-frame joints are made by drilling and cutting plumb, a level timber improves accuracy. While shimming the legs of the sawhorses is a possibility, the best option is to start with a level piece of ground or, even better, a shop floor.

FIND THE ARRIS. With the timber level, use a framing square to find the two sides that are square to each other. These sides become the reference used for layout, and their intersection is known as the arris. It's a good idea to indicate the arris with a chalk mark.

joint and prevent rotation and withdrawal. Modern mechanical fasteners can be used instead of pegs, but in centuries past, they weren't an option.

Here, I'll demonstrate the basic techniques used to cut mortise-and-tenon joints. I start by setting a timber level on sawhorses. I cut the tenon, then the mortise. I wrap up with drawboring, the technique to secure the joint. Before getting started, there are some things to know about timbers.

Choose timber wisely

In timber-framing, the mortise-and-tenon joint is meant to align the timbers in the frame, to pull the timbers tight during assembly, and to keep them tight as the frame shrinks. Some mortise-and-tenon joints are not even pegged if their role is just to register timbers. Some joinery also can bear a considerable weight in compression or shear after the frame is up, but I usually rely on the shoulders or housings around the joints, rather than the tenon itself, to take on this work, especially because the tenons are often tapered a bit to make assembly easier.

A FEW RULES OF THUMB

ONE THING TO KEEP IN MIND is that mortises reduce the strength of any timber, so smaller mortises are better than bigger tenons. Of course, properly sized joinery ultimately is an engineering question, so if in doubt, consult a qualified timber engineer. Here are some general rules.

- Mortises and tenons should typically be one-quarter the width of the timber but never more than one-third.
- The wood remaining on each side of the mortise should be at least the thickness of the tenon, and the peg should penetrate at least that amount on both sides of the tenon.
- The peg diameter should be one-half the thickness of the tenon.

The large dimensions of the timbers themselves create some unique issues. For example, you usually bring the tool to the timber rather than vice versa. Also, as wood dries, it becomes more difficult to work with hand tools, so if you're planning to use seasoned timbers, hardwoods, or a species like Douglas fir that has hard annular rings, you might want to opt for power tools. If you prefer hand tools, you should use an easy-to-work species, such as green eastern white pine.

I recommend that you cut joints as soon as possible after timbers are milled, get the frame raised, and let the timbers shrink after being locked in place. You can accommodate shrinkage in the design and joinery decisions. If you are going to season the timbers, begin by peeling the logs and letting them dry. Wait to mill them square until just before cutting the joints. If you mill timbers square or do the joinery and then store them unassembled for more than a year or so, they may twist so badly that they'll be unusable. Again, use a species that shrinks less, like eastern white pine, rather than hardwoods.

The effects of shrinkage can be particularly pronounced when using large, green timbers that have just come from a sawmill and have not been planed. If you're not using seasoned or planed-to-dimension timbers, you need to be aware of the reference planes of the frame you're building to and to adjust the base of the tools to cut parallel and perpendicular to these planes. This might mean shimming the base of mortises or, if cutting the shoulders or waste from a tenon, being sure to set the depth of the circular saw at the shallowest setting.

Tenons start with the shoulder

When cutting a tenon, always cut the shoulders of the tenon first with a defining kerf, then come in from the end with a chisel. The waste should pop out.

The tenon should be full dimension for at least half the length nearest to the shoulder, but it can be slightly smaller at the outer end where it first engages the mortise so that it enters easily. Taper it about 1/8 in. on the sides and on any nonbearing surfaces. The bottom face of a joist tenon should

KERF THE CUT SHALLOW. To compensate for out-of-square timbers, adjust the blade depth to the shallowest cut. Once the shoulder is cut, kerf out the remaining tenon waste.

NIBBLE YOUR WAY TO THE LINE. Because the grain direction may not run parallel to the tenon, it's a good idea to remove waste gradually with a mallet and chisel, starting well above the line. With most of the kerfed waste removed, turn the chisel and pare across the grain down to the line.

CLEAN UP THE TENON. A block plane works well to chamfer the edges.

THE FRENCH SNAP IS A NEAT TRICK to use when cutting a tenon. (American timber framers learned the trick from French framers, hence the name.) Make two crosscuts, one at the shoulder and one from the other side at the end of the tenon. When you hit the end of the waste block, the timber splits along one of the cheeks of the tenon, saving you a cut. It's a cool trick that dramatically shows how grain can be your friend. However, it's a good idea to make sure the grain is relatively straight before trying it.

not be tapered because it's bearing the load. A 45° chamfer all around, about ¼ in. wide, on the end of the tenon will keep chips from splitting off as the tenon is inserted.

Cut the housing and the mortise

Many mortises have housings to accept the end of the tenoned piece. A housing is one way to hide the effects of shrinkage, and it also provides additional support to the joint. Typically, the author defines the housing with a sawkerf at each side before drilling the mortise.

Whether you use a chain mortiser (photo top right, p. 68) or hand tools, drill the two holes at the ends of the mortise first, then excavate with holes between. Use a drill bit as wide as the mortise will be. Next, chop down across the end grain with a chisel, and then turn the chisel 90° to pare out the parts that have been severed. Repeat as you work your way down into the mortise. Always make the mortise ⅛ in. to ¼ in. deeper than the tenon is long so that the tenon doesn't bottom out in the joint as the timbers dry.

If you're using the surface of the timber as a reference to measure both squareness and depth, the housing tables can be cut slightly concave so that as the timber dries, the tangential shrinkage will make the table flatter, rather than bellying up to push the joint apart.

IN A PERFECT WORLD, TIMBERS ARE PERFECTLY MILLED AND UNIFORM

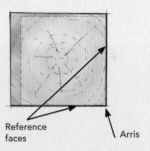

Reference faces

Arris

IN REALITY, TIMBERS USUALLY arrive on site only roughly square and nominally dimensioned. To make layout easier, you can use several methods to correct the material's inconsistencies. The method used here is called the square rule. It's based on the idea that within every irregular, rough-sawn (or hewn) timber, there lies a slightly smaller perfect timber. For example, a 7x7 post may actually measure 7¼ in. by 6¾ in.; it would be laid out as if it were a perfect 6½ in. by 6½ in. On each timber, the straightest two sides that are most square to each other are marked as reference faces. All joinery measurements are made from these faces. Any discrepancies in a timber's dimensions are canceled by cutting a housing or shoulder on the joint's mating surface that reduces the parts to the perfect timber size.

KERF THE HOUSING FIRST. After marking the mortise and housing, cut the outer edges of the housing. If using a circular saw, be sure to set the blade to the shallowest depth of the square-rule layout.

DEFINE THE MORTISE. A chain mortiser is like a mini-chainsaw set up for plunge cuts. Begin at the ends, then cut out the middle of the mortise.

PLAN FOR WOOD SHRINKAGE. It's best to make the housing surface or table slightly concave so that the joint stays tight as the wood shrinks.

CLEAN OUT THE HOUSING. After making a series of kerfs across the housing, pare down the line with a chisel.

Draw the joint tight with an offset peg

Peg holes should be drilled perpendicular or slightly off angle to the face, and all the way through the mortised member. It's best to start from the face closest to the tenon. Some timber framers drill the joints for pegs all at once after the frame is assembled and pulled together on site, but those joints will never get any tighter and may open over time. When pegs are driven through a joint, the drilled hole shouldn't really be straight. Instead, the peg holes should be slightly offset, or drawbored, to pull the joint tight during assembly and to keep the joint tight as the timbers settle. By offsetting the peg hole in the tenon a bit, the peg bends slightly to pull the tenon into the mortise and to act like a spring for maintaining tension as the timbers season.

PREVENT BLOWOUT. Because the auger bit is pulled through the timber by its screwhead, it will stop cutting when the tip emerges. If you pull up while drilling, you won't bore through the other side.

MARK THE OFFSET. Fully insert the tenon into the mortise, and lightly mark the tenon with the drill bit. Pull out the tenon, and mark an offset of a light ⅛ in. toward the tenon's shoulder. Drill the tenon's peg hole in the offset location.

LOCK THE JOINT. After fully reseating the tenon, drive a tapered drawbore peg into the hole, which draws together the joint.

Framing with a Crane

BY JIM ANDERSON

The other day, I kept an eye on the three-man framing crew working across the street. Two of the guys spent the day in the mud, hauling material for the second floor into the house. When my crew was rolling up for the day, the other crew had carried most of the lumber inside the house but still needed to pull it up to the second floor. It cost this crew about $300* in labor just to get the studs in the door.

I'd have hired a crane for this job and moved all that lumber in about an hour, which would have cost me $125. Even if there were no money savings, saving wear and tear on my body and those of my crew would make the crane worthwhile.

I started to think of better ways to use a crane six years ago when my brother and I went into business framing houses. We carried most of the material the hard way, but we hired a crane to set the steel I-beams.

It occurred to us that although the crane company charged us for a full hour of crane time, setting those three steel beams took 20 minutes. With that realization, we decided to fill the other 40 minutes of that hour by using the crane as our laborer.

My brother has moved on, and I now have my own two-helper crew. I still call in a crane several times for an average house. Where I work, in the suburbs south of Denver, Colorado, cranes are pretty common. The ones that I hire usually have no move-in fee, just a one-hour minimum charge of about $125*.

Preparation Is key

Before the crane arrives, I try to ensure that the lumber is dumped fairly close to the house, but not where it will be in the crane's way. When the crane does arrive, I discuss the sequence of the lift with the operator and crew. For efficiency, everybody has to know what's coming next.

One crew member stays near the material to rig it to the crane. The other two stay near where the material will be installed. To avoid confusion, one of these carpenters is the designated signaler (see the sidebar on p. 74), whereas the other jockeys the load into position.

Most of the houses that my crew and I frame have three to five steel beams holding up the first floor. These beams are the first things that the crane sets. We either have the Lally columns cut to length or have ready temporary posts. Long 2×4s are on hand to brace the I-beam to the mudsills once it's in place.

We set the beam that's farthest back in the building first, then move sequentially to the front. This process avoids swinging anything over set beams, eliminating the chance of dropping one beam and taking out two.

We stack any scrap from the basement on a piece of sheathing. We lift this scrap out of the hole with the crane and swing it right over to the Dumpster.

Any built-up wood or laminated veneer lumber (LVL) beams are nailed together, and any necessary

hangers are installed beforehand. As we work back to front, I set these beams in sequence with the steel.

The stacks of floor joists are next, and after they have all been set on the foundation walls, we move as much of the material as we can closer to the house. We put the lifts of floor sheathing on top of 2×4 stickers about 3 ft. from the front of the house,

allowing room to work but putting it within easy reach. Then we use the crane to move the rim-joist material to the top of the stacks of sheathing. We cut the rims here, using the sheathing stacks as 1,500-lb. sawhorses.

A WELL-RIGGED JOB GOES SMOOTHLY AND SAFELY

THREE KINDS OF RIGGING EQUIPMENT GET us through any house. The most frequently used are nylon straps, followed by steel cables and four-chain rigging.

NYLON STRAPS ARE RIGGED IN TWO WAYS

CRADLE-RIGGING RUNS THE STRAP UNDER THE LOAD IN A U-SHAPE. Great for trusses and walls, they should never be used to lift studs or joists overhead.

CHOKE-RIGGING TIGHTENS AS THE CRANE LIFTS. Choke rigs limit movement within lifts such as studs or sheathing, and they keep beams from slipping out of single straps. To avoid excessive flexing, I-joists (right) are choked in about one-quarter of the joists' length from each end.

CABLES AND FOUR-CHAIN RIGS ARE LESS COMMON

FOUR-CHAIN RIGS RAISE THE ROOF. Hooked to the crane with a ring, each chain can be snubbed to a length that will enable a preassembled truss rack to fly level.

STEEL CABLES CAN DAMAGE THE EDGES OF MATERIAL. They're limited to raising single trusses and sliding under material dropped directly onto the ground so that it can be raised enough to get a strap below.

Have the garage walls ready to lift

Most of the houses we frame have three-car garages with one single door and one double door. A typical garage-door wall is 30 ft. long and 10 ft. tall, with an 18-ft. and a 9-ft. double-LVL header. I never want to lift a wall like this by hand. Before the crane arrives, we frame and stand the sidewalls that we can easily lift by hand. We also frame the front wall but leave it on the ground for the crane to lift.

The crane lifts the wall and swings it to the garage foundation. As it gets close, we guide the anchor bolts into the holes we've drilled for them in the bottom plate, then down the wall. Now the crane holds the wall in place as we nail the corners, tie in the plates, and nail on some braces. With the wall set and braced, we give the "all finished" signal and send the crane home. This entire lift—I-beams to garage wall—usually takes only about an hour.

THE STEEL IS READY TO GO WHEN THE CRANE ARRIVES. The wood sills to which the joists will be nailed are already attached to the steel, and the joist locations are marked.

Better than carrying material to the second floor

After we've framed the first-floor walls, we build a section of the second floor to serve as a staging area for our next lift. This area is usually a corner that's, say, 500 sq. ft. to 800 sq. ft. We also frame most of the walls around this area before placing any material here. This prep work saves having to move lumber to make room to frame the walls.

Once this staging area is done, I call the crane again to lift the studs, the plates, and the sheathing for the second-floor walls, as well as the balance of the second-floor joists and beams.

Full lifts of studs or of OSB sheathing are pretty heavy loads that should never be set in the middle of a joist span. We set lifts of material on 2×4s to spread the weight and to leave room to remove the straps once the crane lets go of the load. We always set our material on or near the main bearing beams and walls below the floor. If for some reason a load must be set midspan, we split it into smaller bundles that can be spread out. We sometimes build a temporary wall below the floor to help spread the load to more joists.

During this lift, we set any second-floor steel or built-up LVLs. Commonly, there is a beam that runs between two walls, each end supported by posts made of studs or by Lally columns enclosed within pockets in the wall. Although we frame these walls with their top plates uninterrupted, we leave the posts out until we set the beam.

GETTING THE CRANE TO DO WHAT YOU NEED

THERE ARE STANDARD HAND SIGNALS that all crane operators and the people who hire them should know. In addition, three rules and a suggestion can make communication a sure thing.

1. Keep your signal in one place.

2. If you can't see the operator through a maze of studs, trusses, or bracing, the operator can't see you. Make eye contact, and then make your signals in front of your face.

3. If your gloves and clothing are of similar colors, make your signals away from your body where the operator can see. Another way to communicate with the operator is with two-way radios.

TO RAISE OR LOWER A LOAD, POINT UP OR DOWN AND ROTATE YOUR FINGER. To move the load slowly, put your opposite hand above or below your signal, as if you're pointing at your palm. When the load is down, a quick circle with the hand signals that all is clear and that the hook can be dropped to free the load.

RAISE LOAD

RAISE LOAD SLOWLY

RAISING OR LOWERING THE BOOM MOVES A LOAD TOWARD OR AWAY FROM THE CRANE. Thumb up moves the load toward the crane. Thumb down moves the load away. Either gesture pointed at the opposite palm means to go slowly. To move the load without raising or lowering it, point your thumb up or down while opening and closing your fist.

LOWER BOOM

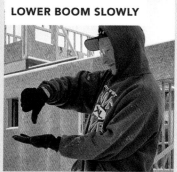

LOWER BOOM SLOWLY

SWINGING THE BOOM IS AS SIMPLE AS POINTING WHERE YOU NEED TO MOVE THE LOAD. Finally, the most important signal is a closed fist, for stopping the crane. Additional signals are used to guide the larger cranes used on commercial jobs, but these six signals and their variations should get you through most residential work.

SWING BOOM

STOP CRANE

A CRANE MAKES SHORT WORK OF RAISING TOP-HEAVY GARAGE WALLS. Once the wall is set over the anchor bolts, the crane steadies the wall until it's tied to the others and braced.

BE PREPARED FOR THE CRANE'S SECOND VISIT. This second-floor staging area is framed to provide storage space for crane-lifted studs and sheathing. Because stored material would otherwise be in the way, the author also frames the walls before the crane arrives.

To set a beam that runs between walls, we pull down one end and slide it far enough into its pocket that the beam's other end clears the wall plate. Then we have the crane operator lower the beam, and we seesaw it into place. With the crane snugging the beam to the underside of the top plates, we tip in the supporting columns.

Raising balloon-frame walls

The only first-floor walls we don't lift by hand are any tall, balloon-frame walls, such as those of rooms with very high ceilings. We frame and sheathe these walls with the other walls but leave them flat until the crane comes again. For safety alone, lifting these walls is worth hiring a crane.

With the wall's bottom plate on its layout line, we secure it to the deck about every 4 ft. using pieces of the steel strap that bands lifts of lumber. This strap acts as a hinge, keeping the wall from kicking out during the lift.

We stop the lift about a third of the way up to attach the braces that will steady the raised wall. These braces go about two-thirds of the way up the wall. Once the braces are nailed to the wall, we stand it up the rest of the way, then plumb and brace it before unhooking the crane.

The final lift sets the roof trusses

With the second-floor walls plumbed and lined, it's time for the crane again. This time it will lift our sheathing, roof-framing lumber, prebuilt truss racks, and any single trusses. First, we swing up the roof sheathing and set it in three or four spots on the second floor. Then we send up the lumber for framing dormers and valleys. This lumber is usually set in the main hallway of the upper level, where we have room to maneuver long pieces up into the roof framing.

When the site and truss design allow, we assemble, sheathe, and brace the trusses into 6-ft. to 18-ft. roof sections on the ground. We can set a simple gable roof, preassembled into two to three sections, in about a half-hour.

Our total crane time on an average house is about 4½ hours. In most cases, we hire a 3-ton crane. These cranes have 90-ft. booms that will reach about 60 ft. with most loads that we see in residential construction. Only once have we needed a larger crane. If you aren't sure of the size crane that you need, call the crane company and describe your lift. They'll know.

There are two other advantages to hiring a crane. The first is safety. We once helped another framer attempt to raise a large wall by hand. It got away from us, pinning one of my employees below. Added to his pain and disability is the fact that my worker's comp premiums went up 50 percent.

The second advantage is job-site security. Using a crane to lift material into the house as soon as possible makes it less accessible to thieves. They'll likely head across the street to the house where the lumber is still sitting where it was delivered, conveniently right next to the curb.

*Prices are from 2001.

CRANE SAFETY IS MOSTLY COMMON SENSE

CRANES OFFER IMMEDIATE SAFETY benefits by lifting heavy loads that you might otherwise attempt to manhandle. And by reducing the repetitive toting and lifting of construction, they can foster long-term benefits in the form of healthy backs, knees, and shoulders.

However, cranes bring with them some danger, simply because they carry heavy things overhead. Obeying three rules should get you home safe after every day of crane work.

- Wear a hard hat: OSHA requires it.

- Don't stand under suspended loads.

- Don't become trapped between the load and a wall or a drop-off. A sudden horizontal movement of the load could crush you or send you flying.

TWO STRAPS ARE USED TO RAISE TALL WALLS. Had there been no windows, the crew would have cut small holes in the sheathing for the straps.

WITH THE WALLS PARTIALLY RAISED AND SHORED FOR SAFETY, the braces are tacked so that they can pivot as the wall rises.

Bringing Advanced Framing to Your Job Site

BY DANNY KELLY

Most houses have a lot more lumber in the walls than is really needed. All of that extra wood not only increases the costs but also adds to thermal bridging and steals room from insulation.

Advanced framing aims to eliminate any lumber that isn't critical to the structure. Green-building programs award points for using advanced-framing techniques, which is great, but that's not why my firm does it. We do it because it allows us to use 2x6 studs and to install more insulation for about the same price as 2x4 walls. Also, the Department of Energy says a home with advanced framing will cost 5% less to heat and cool, which is a lot of money over the life of the structure.

Our path to advanced framing was incremental. We started about five years ago, when we began eliminating redundant jacks and cripples. Then we switched to 24-in. centers, two-stud corners, and ladder blocking at interior-wall intersections. These simple steps reduced the number of studs in the walls by 50%.

Where do you start the layout for stacked framing?

PICK A CORNER. Start the layout at a corner where all the framing elements can be stacked from the mudsill to the rafters. An advantage of using a single top plate is that the stud layout on the top plate also can be used for joists or rafters.

Is there enough backing for trim?

INSTALL NAILERS FOR WINDOWS. Add 2x2s to the king studs to provide nailing for windows, siding, and exterior casing. Biscuits can reinforce corners on wide casing. Depending on the interior trim, you may have to do this for interior casing as well.

LONG WALLS ARE HARD TO LIFT. Advanced-framed walls are wobbly compared to conventionally framed walls. Even though they're lighter, you'll still need extra hands on deck. Small crews can frame walls in shorter segments to keep them under control as they're raised.

Once my crew felt comfortable with these changes, we made a switch to single top plates. This requires the framing members to be stacked within 1 in. of each other, creating an uninterrupted structural load path from the roof to the foundation. We look for a corner where we can stack from the mudsill to the rafters, and we start our joist, stud, and rafter layouts there. One potential problem with using single top plates is that precut studs create a wall that's 1½ in. shorter than typical. This isn't a big deal with 8-ft. walls, because you can simply buy 8-ft. studs and cut them down, but with 9-ft. walls, you have to cut down 10-ft. studs, which generates a lot of waste. Our solution is to cut the drywall a little shorter and use standard precut 9-ft. studs.

When the engineer allows, we also eliminate the conventional headers and use the band joist as a header. If the band joist alone is structurally insufficient, we install a header between the band joist and the floor joists, which allows more insulation in the wall. If a header must go in the wall, we cover it with rigid foam on the exterior and use header hangers to eliminate jack studs.

We've found only one real drawback to advanced framing: With less lumber in the wall, there are fewer places to mount outlets, switches, and cabinets, so we often have to add blocking. It's important to communicate with your subs about this early so that these details can be worked out ahead of time.

ELIMINATE EXTRA STUDS. When possible, eliminate extra jack and cripple studs by locating windows and doors so that at least one side of the opening falls within the normal stud layout. Be sure to leave room for casing, and consider the final elevation when moving doors and windows.

BRACE WALLS WELL. As with conventional framing, begin plumbing and lining walls at corners, then at intersections. Unlike with conventional framing, you may need extra bracing to make up for more wobbly walls.

How do you fasten drywall at inside corners?

LADDER TEES AT INTERSECTING WALLS. Ladder tees reduce thermal bridging and use up small pieces of lumber that might otherwise go to waste. Locate the tees so that they line up with trim elements and drywall seams.

What do you use instead of a second top plate?

INVEST IN A CONNECTOR NAILER. In lieu of a second plate, intersecting wall sections are joined with metal tie plates. Each plate requires 32 nails. Assuming each fastener takes several seconds to hand-nail, this nailer paid for itself a long time ago.

STRING FOR STRAIGHT WALLS. Without a second top plate, advanced-framed walls built with warped lumber will look wavy, so use the straightest lumber possible. Stringlines and bracing can help to correct any problems.

USE HEADER HANGERS. In areas where you need conventional headers, use steel header hangers to eliminate jack studs.

MOVE HEADERS INTO THE FLOOR FRAME. Window and door headers generally aren't needed in gable-end walls. Where headers are needed, the band joists (or engineered rim board) often can satisfy header requirements, as over these gable-wall windows.

STACKED FRAMING TRANSFERS THE LOAD
Aligned studs, joists, and rafters allow you to eliminate the second top plate in framed walls. Stacked framing also makes it easier to rough in pipes and ducts.

How big are headers?

SKIP HEADERS WHEN POSSIBLE. Openings in non-load-bearing walls don't need headers. In spots where you do need them, size them appropriately, and leave as much room as possible for insulation by using hangers or by moving the header into the floor above.

BE ON THE LOOKOUT FOR PROBLEMS. The author walks the site nearly every day. He marks unnecessary framing members for removal and indicates where additional blocking is needed.

Framing for Efficiency

BY STEVE BACZEK

The frame of a Passive House may not be as exciting as the thick layers of insulation, the high-tech mechanical systems, or the triple-glazed windows, but it plays a very important supporting role—pun intended—in achieving success.

I chose every component of the framing package in this house with care, and for a specific reason. The exterior sheathing provides airtightness, the double-stud walls and raised-heel roof trusses are a cost-effective means of supporting or containing above-average levels of insulation, and the floor trusses easily span the open floor plan and provide plenty of room for the many ducts necessary for the ventilation system and supporting mechanicals.

Two walls, two air barriers

The chief function of the double-stud walls is to hold insulation. Measuring 14 in. from the interior face of the 2x4 inner wall to the exterior face of the 2x6 outer wall, the wall assembly provides a 5-in. thermal break between halves.

DOUBLE-STUD WALLS. The interior frame provided the typical mounting surface for fixtures and finishes, but it also served as a barrier to contain the cavity insulation before the final wallboard was installed.

MULTIPURPOSE COMPONENTS

ROOF TRUSSES. Because the attic won't be used for anything but insulation, raised-heel roof trusses were a quick and cost-efficient means of putting a lid on this house and of providing a way to hang and finish the ceiling air barrier before partition walls went in.

FLOOR TRUSSES. Open-web floor trusses offer long spans and the ability to run mechanicals between the first and second floors—a saving grace in a house where the attic is off-limits and there is no basement.

OUTSIDE FRAME. The outside frame supports most of the floor load and all of the roof load. It also holds part of the primary air barrier and, with the help of diagonal bracing, provides the necessary wind-shear resistance for this coastal site.

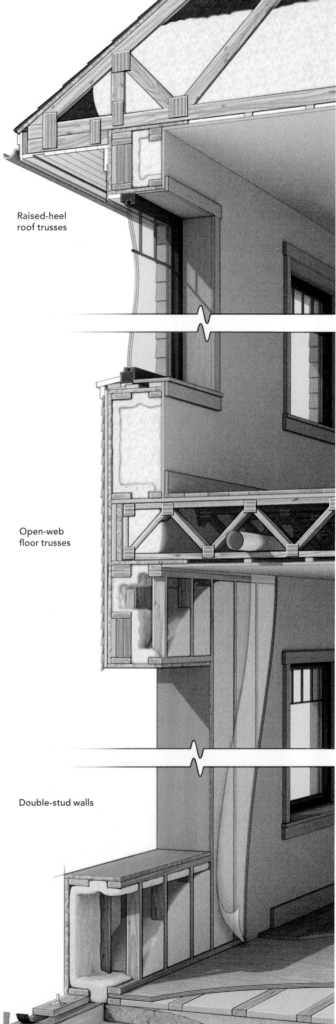

Raised-heel
roof trusses

Open-web
floor trusses

Double-stud walls

In addition to the taped sheathing seams and the picture-frame-style application of Tremco acoustical sealant, the wall is redundantly air-sealed with a 4-in.-thick coat of closed-cell foam sprayed against the inside face of the sheathing. The remainder of the cavity is filled with 10 in. of dry, dense-packed cellulose, bringing the wall assembly to an overall thermal resistance of about R-52.

Some energy-conscious builders and architects might wonder why anybody would design a building that represents the height of energy efficiency, and specify walls with 2x6 studs spaced 16 in. on center and structural headers over every window—details that fly in the face of advanced-framing techniques.

Given that these walls are thermally broken by the cavity between the inner and outer stud walls, the only advantage to framing with studs set on 24-in. centers would be a small cost savings in lumber. But on this house, which is located in a coastal high-wind zone, that small savings would have been offset by the additional structural measures required of a wall 24 in. on center.

For the headers, all of which are thermally broken with a piece of 2-in.-thick rigid foam, I have found that consistency pays even if it results in a minor energy penalty. I try to minimize decisions for the builder to increase the likelihood that the things I need to be done right will be done right. Also, for what it's worth, the high-performance triple-glazed windows necessary in a Passive House are two to three times the weight of a typical double-glazed window, so a robust window frame is a good thing.

At the top of each wall, bridging the gap between the interior and exterior stud walls, is a rip of ¾-in. plywood, which has a couple of duties. First, it caps and isolates the cavity space of the double-stud wall. Second, it overhangs the interior wall plate, providing a means to connect the interior ceiling to the wall assembly, maintaining the continuity of the air barrier. A third function is one I hadn't planned for but that the builders found very useful: a walking surface. By attaching bracing below the plywood

flange, the builders were able to walk the walls easily while installing the floor and roof trusses.

Strong, wide-open floor framing

One of my goals in designing a successful Passive House is to get as much of the structural load from the floors and roof as possible to the outside of the house. This allows me to keep an open floor plan, which is helpful in moving conditioned air around the house. To achieve this open floor plan, I needed engineered floor joists, which can span longer distances than dimensional lumber.

Although it's largely heated by the sun in the winter, a Passive House still relies on mechanical systems. In addition to the standard plumbing and electrical, this house has lots of ductwork for ventilation. Without a basement or conditioned attic, just about everything has to run through the floor joists that support the second level.

This combined need for a long span and room for lots of mechanicals made open-web floor trusses an easy choice. They are cost-effective and sturdy, and they eliminate concerns about the placement of penetrations or the need for mechanical chases.

This attic is for insulation

Because the attic will hold 24 in. of loose-fill cellulose, I didn't even attempt to provide storage or living space up there. Forfeiting any claim to the attic made roof trusses an easy choice compared to a traditional stick-built roof, and allowed me to get the house dried in and prepped for the uppermost portion of the primary air barrier: the ceilings.

To ensure that this ceiling air barrier—a layer of veneer-plastered blueboard—would be continuous, the plaster installers hung and finished the ceiling before any interior partition walls were framed. That approach not only eliminated the hundreds of linear feet of joints between top plates and ceiling joists—all of which are weak points in an air barrier—but it made the hanger's job easier because full sheets of blueboard could be used.

THE CONSTRUCTION SEQUENCE IS GUIDED BY BLOWER-DOOR TESTS

THE AIRTIGHTNESS REQUIREMENT FOR PASSIVE HOUSE certification is less than or equal to 0.6 air changes per hour at –50 Pa (AC H50). This number can also be expressed as 177 cubic feet per minute at –50 Pa (cfm50). I prefer to use the cfm figures because the larger number makes any changes in performance easier to track.

Test result: 177 cfm50

PHASE 1
PRIMARY AIR BARRIER

The primary air barrier in this house is formed by the slab, the exterior sheathing, and the plastered ceilings below each roofline. Backed up with a thick, continuous bead of Tremco acousti-

Test result: 83 cfm50

cal sealant at all seam edges, the 7/16-in.-thick Zip System OSB was chosen because of its butyl-based seam-sealing tape, which partners with the water- and air-resistive barrier that's bonded to the exterior side of each sheet. The rough openings at windows and doors are left uncut so that the builders can test the airtightness of the shell before moving to the next step of the process.

PHASE 2
SECONDARY AIR BARRIER

A 4-in.-thick coat of closed-cell polyurethane-foam insulation is sprayed on the inner face of the wall sheathing. Running continuously from the subslab insulation to the top plates, the foam performs a couple

Test result: 46 cfm50

of functions. First, it acts as a secondary air barrier should there be any air leakage through the sheathing seams or the acoustical sealant. Second, with an insulation value of roughly R-27, it ensures that the inner surface of the sheathing remains above the dewpoint, eliminating the risk of condensation in the extrathick wall assembly.

PHASE 3
WINDOWS AND DOORS

Even a house with the best windows and doors in the world, installed perfectly, is leakier than a house without any openings. For that reason, once the sheathing has been cut

Test result: 106 cfm50

away at rough openings and the windows and doors are in place, the air-leakage numbers will creep up slightly. Also, because most penetrations should have been made at this point, this test result should be a fairly accurate prediction of the final result once the house is complete.

PHASE 4
INSULATION AND MECHANICALS

With the more-delicate control functions handled as close to the outside face of the building as possible, the space between the outer and inner stud walls and the space in the attic offer an

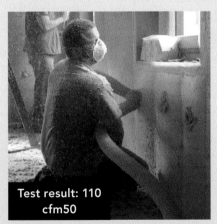

Test result: 110 cfm50

opportunity for more-cost-effective insulation to provide the bulk of the thermal resistance. Cellulose insulation is packed into the walls to a density of 3.6 lb. per sq. ft., adding R-37 to the overall thermal resistance of the wall assembly. In the attic, loose-fill cellulose is piled to a depth of 24 in., providing an R-92 insulated lid above the ceiling air barrier of the house. At this stage, minor leakage typically stems from final work on mechanical rough-ins and other last-minute tweaks.

Exploring the Benefits of Engineered Floor Joists

BY CHRIS ERMIDES

I t used to be that architects and designers were limited by floor-framing choices; dimensional lumber was the only thing available. Depending on species and age, a 2x8, 2x10, or 2x12 might require supporting beams or bearing walls, both of which could limit design possibilities. Large, uninterrupted spaces were complicated to design and build.

Engineered floor-framing options such as wood I-joists and floor trusses, however, can span greater lengths with fewer caveats, yielding open spaces easily accessible to designers and framers. Both I-joists and floor trusses minimize or eliminate potential engineering problems and in the end—despite the added upfront cost—might even save money. Engineered wood joists and trusses are easier to specify, are more stable than dimensional lumber, and are easier to install.

Load affects the top and bottom of floor joists

I-joists were developed to meet the demands of open floor plans. Architects needed a material that could clear-span areas larger than dimensional lumber without complicated engineering. When they arrived on the market in 1969, I-joists were made of a plywood web capped with top and bottom flanges. Those flanges were either laminated-veneer lumber (LVL), solid lumber, or strand lumber. Today, those webs are made of oriented strand board (OSB), while the flange options are limited to LVLs and sawn lumber.

One advantage I-joists have over dimensional lumber is consistency and stability. Dimensional lumber can vary in width from board to board, and even end to end. It shrinks over time, and framers have to be mindful of splits, checks, twists, and crowns in every board. Setting a single joist becomes a multistep process. Also, the possibility of shrinkage means potential drywall cracks and uneven, wavy ceilings.

I-JOISTS

I-JOISTS NOW MAKE UP MORE THAN 50% of the floor-joist market. They're strong, lightweight, stable, and more versatile than dimensional lumber. Longer spans, varying depths, and a range of flange widths provide builders with options for dialing in price and performance. They're available from national and regional manufacturers through local lumberyards. Price varies by location.

OSB has replaced plywood, the original web material used by most manufacturers, each of which makes its own OSB webs to ensure the strength and quality of the joist. Proprietary OSB webbing is often designed to resist moisture, which can pose a serious threat to the integrity of the flange-to-web bond.

The flanges are made of either solid dimensional lumber or LVL material. LVL flanges are made up of thin wood veneers, which manufacturers claim means that they're more stable. Wooden flanges are as strong as most LVL flanges, but they are more susceptible to movement from expansion and contraction. It's important to note, however, that expansion and contraction are minimal because these flanges are attached to stable OSB webbing. Manufacturers of solid-wood flange types maintain that those flanges are as stable and resource-efficient as LVL flanges, and more economical as well.

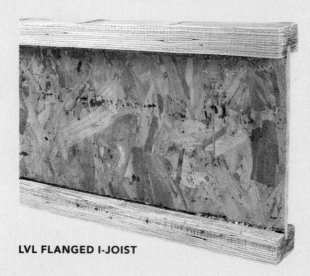

LVL FLANGED I-JOIST

SAWN-LUMBER FLANGED I-JOIST

PROS
- Available in many sizes and configurations so that performance can be somewhat customized.
- Lightweight so that they're easy to maneuver around the job site.
- Install like dimensional lumber, which most framers are familiar with.
- Span and load ratings are predetermined, so layout can be reconfigured on site as needed.
- Dimensionally consistent and stable.

CONS
- OSB-to-flange connection is susceptible to damage if exposed to excessive moisture.
- Not structurally stable until bracing and/or floor sheathing is installed.
- Web stiffeners are required at point loads and when hangers are used, which means more time to install.

The most exploitable advantage I-joists have over dimensional lumber, though, is strength. At first glance, it's tough to imagine that a 3/8-in.-thick web of OSB capped with 2x2 blocks of wood could be as strong as a solid piece of lumber. To accept that fact, you need to understand how load stresses are distributed within an I-joist.

As a load bears down on an I-joist, the load stresses mainly the top and the bottom flanges. The wood fibers on the top flange are compressed, while the fibers on the bottom flange are stretched. The fibers near mid-depth, however, are virtually unaffected.

This is why it's OK to drill holes along the center—and also why you can't notch the top and bottom of any joists. Notches remove wood fiber from the joist areas that need it most.

Builders such as Michael Chandler in Raleigh, N.C., like I-joists for their strength and value, but also for their sustainable qualities. "My goal is to build houses that will last more than 100 years," Chandler says, "and I want to do so with minimal impact on the environment." The fact that I-joists use far less wood than dimensional lumber is a big benefit for many builders.

I-joists offer builders flexibility

I-joist manufacturers have figured out a way to optimize the physics involved in the way bending stresses are distributed within a joist, and they have designed a product that puts wood where it's needed most and removes it where it's needed least. The result is a stronger, straighter, and lighter joist than dimensional lumber.

Save for a few necessary stiffeners, I-joists install similarly to dimensional lumber, and they offer builders similar flexibility to dimensional joists. Because allowable spans are set by I-joist manufacturers, a framer can move a layout as necessary if changes need to be made after the joists are delivered. I-joists can be doubled for added strength

or moved to make room for plumbing and other mechanicals. I-joists also offer more options for drilling holes.

Manufacturers such as iLevel offer free software to help designers and builders customize performance. To help builders achieve desired floor performance, most manufacturers offer a selection of I-joists with variations in flange size, web thickness, and depth.

Floor trusses are custom joists

Given their strength, their efficient use of materials, and their open-web design, wood floor trusses are sustainably built and offer benefits to builders, subs, and even homeowners. Truss manufacturers can take a set of plans and customize the truss designs down to details of concentrated load placement and utility chases (pp. 92–93).

Aside from their design characteristics, trusses are easy to install—as long as framers follow the truss manufacturer's placement diagrams. Lisa Biggin, construction manager for Habitat for Humanity in Newburgh, N.Y., likes trusses for several reasons. "I need to clear-span distances that would require structural supports for I-joists or dimensional lumber," she says. "The added cost for those supports and columns would make the floor system more expensive than just the cost of floor trusses." Biggin also likes how easily floor trusses install. Everything is precut and ready to go, so even Habitat volunteers who don't have framing experience can handle the installation without a glitch.

Biggin points out that proper planning and site management are the keys to capitalizing on the cost/ time benefit of using trusses. Training installers and subs about the dos and don'ts goes a long way toward avoiding costly mistakes. An entire set of trusses can be installed and sheathed before anyone realizes that they've all been placed upside down; it has happened before. Paying attention to the manufacturer's instructions is important.

FLOOR TRUSSES

OPEN-WEB FLOOR TRUSSES are gaining popularity, especially in custom homes. They're lightweight, strong, and capable of making long spans. Builders like them because they can be fully customized. For example, multiple live and dead loads can be designed along a set of trusses, eliminating the need for bearing walls or beams. It's also possible to create utility chases up to 24 in. wide at any desired location. Open webs make running wire and pipe easier, but having a dedicated chase makes work easier for subs. A truss designer can spec a set of trusses to desired spans, deflection, point loads, and bearing capacity while taking into account the materials that will be added later. The bottom line: Performance is highly customizable.

Trusses are available mostly through regional manufacturers and local lumberyards. Prices depend on design and location.

Stress-rated 2x pine is used for both top and bottom chords, as well as for webbing. The chords tend to run a higher grade, usually No. 2 or better. Web lumber is stress-rated as well, although it isn't usually as high grade. This is where manufacturers keep costs under control; higher-rated wood is used where it's needed according to the load design for a particular truss.

Web members join to top and bottom chords by heavy-gauge steel nailing plates. These plates come in various sizes and gauges that are pressed into the wood at each joint by a large roller or hydraulic press.

TOP CHORD-BEARING TRUSS

BOTTOM CHORD-BEARING TRUSS

PROS

- Customized layout and truss design with an engineer's stamp means less time and worry for the builder.
- Customized performance means guaranteed results.
- Utilities are easy to run and are accessible later, saving time and money.
- Easy and fast to install.
- No additional bearing blocking is needed.
- Wide bearing surface makes for faster, more accurate subfloor installation.

CONS

- Customization means that layout changes can't be made in the field.
- All layout/structural changes have to be approved by an engineer and might require new trusses.
- Framers unfamiliar with them can install them improperly: upside down, front to back, or in the wrong order.

HOW ENGINEERED JOISTS WORK

JOIST SPANS DEPEND ON THE STRENGTH AND STIFFNESS of the member and the amount of load it is required to carry. Deflection, or the degree to which a joist flexes under the design load, is commonly taken to be the main factor in the way a floor performs. Live loads (such as the weight of furniture and people) and dead loads (the weight of actual materials) are both used in calculating deflection.

The International Residential Code (IRC) limits floor-joist deflection to span/360 (where span is measured in inches) for live loads in living spaces (40 psf) and in sleeping areas (30 psf). The higher the denominator, the lower the deflection and, generally, the better the performance. Although this might generally be true, deflection isn't the only variable to consider in a floor's performance. While deflection is important, a number of other factors can affect floor performance. According to Tim Debelius, a spokesman for joist manufacturer iLevel (www.ilevel.com), a floor can have a deflection rating as high as span/720 and still feel bouncy, or a low span/280 and feel firm. Joist depth plays an obvious role in performance. The deeper the joist, the stiffer the floor will likely be. Ceilings installed on the bottom of a floor system and other materials also affect performance. Ceilings, for example, help to brace the bottoms of joists, tying them all together and limiting their ability to shift left to right. Strongbacks, blocking, and flooring material matter, too. Factors including the floor system's weight (dead load) and the elasticity of these materials all contribute to a floor's performance.

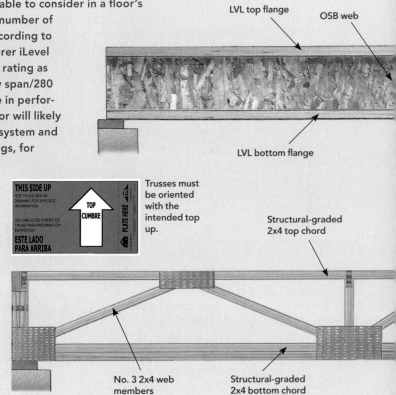

LVL top flange

OSB web

LVL bottom flange

THIS SIDE UP
SEE TRUSS DESIGN DRAWING FOR SPECIFIC INFORMATION

VEA DIBUJO DE DISEÑO DE TRUSS PARA INFORMACIÓN ESPECÍFICA

ESTE LADO PARA ARRIBA

TOP CUMBRE

PLATE HERE

Trusses must be oriented with the intended top up.

Structural-graded 2x4 top chord

No. 3 2x4 web members

Structural-graded 2x4 bottom chord

Open webs benefit everyone

For shallower depths and shorter spans, floor trusses are more expensive than I-joists, but as Biggin points out, comparing the cost of I-joists to trusses without considering the big picture can be misleading. Builders who swear by trusses like them most for their open webs, which make mechanical contractors' work a lot easier.

"My subs are able to run plumbing, wiring, and any other utility without drilling holes," says Arkansas builder Gary Striegler. "They're through the job site faster, which moves the whole project

DRILL HOLES WITH CAUTION

I-joist flanges and webbing each play a crucial role in the way load is distributed within the member. Modifying flanges in any way could result in structural failure. Drilling holes in the webbing outside of the manufacturer's recommendations could result in structural failure as well. See the manufacturer's installation information for specific guidance on hole sizing and spacing requirements. Below are examples of some requirements.

DON'T CHANGE A THING

Because of the way trusses are engineered, every piece has a predetermined role in how it performs. Therefore, any modifications, however slight, affect the entire truss and could result in structural failure. Don't trim the ends, add point loads without an engineer's approval, or cut, notch, and drill through webs, plates, or chords. Also, look for installation guidance from tags like the ones shown here.

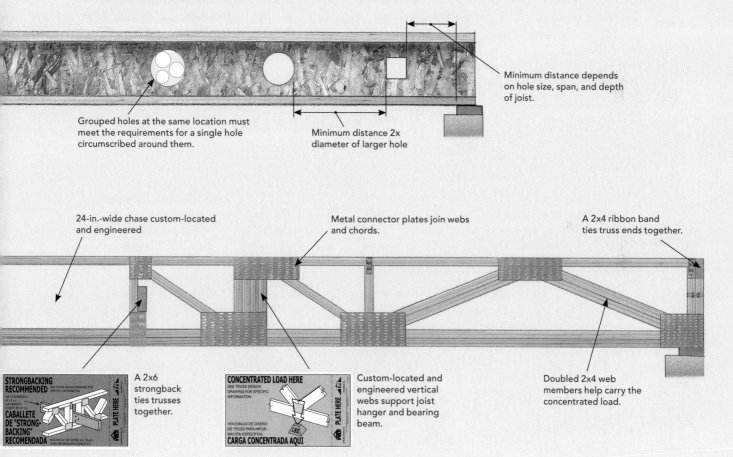

Grouped holes at the same location must meet the requirements for a single hole circumscribed around them.

Minimum distance 2x diameter of larger hole

Minimum distance depends on hole size, span, and depth of joist.

24-in.-wide chase custom-located and engineered

Metal connector plates join webs and chords.

A 2x4 ribbon band ties truss ends together.

A 2x6 strongback ties trusses together.

Custom-located and engineered vertical webs support joist hanger and bearing beam.

Doubled 2x4 web members help carry the concentrated load.

along more quickly." For Striegler and other builders, saving time for subcontractors translates into saving money for the whole project.

Michael Chandler uses floor trusses for the second floors of the houses he builds. Chandler's truss designer allocates a section of the truss for a utility chase. Using this design allows Chandler's subs to keep their work clean and neat. The greatest benefit for Chandler, though, is from an energy-efficiency standpoint. "It's important to have all HVAC ductwork within the building envelope. Trusses provide a place for ductwork in a conditioned environment, not an attic," Chandler says.

Dialing in performance is a tricky equation

It used to be that builders didn't have many options or resources available for customizing floor performance. Sawn-lumber floor joists were typically the same grade, size, and spacing required for the longest span within the system. With I-joists and trusses, builders can design and install floors that maximize performance based on each part of the house and the way it will be used.

Living spaces such as hallways don't require the same deflection rating as sleeping spaces, for example. No matter how spaces feel underfoot,

builders want to ensure that floors don't make a sound, that tile doesn't crack, and that drywall doesn't pop. Joist sizing and strength can vary in different parts of a house.

Open-web floor trusses play a large role here. A builder can hand plans to the truss manufacturer with specs such as desired deflection, floor-material selections, and location of utility chases. In about a week, the builder gets a floor-framing plan that's fully customized and guaranteed to perform.

Custom-home builders such as Mike Guertin in Rhode Island like this level of customization and

KEY INSTALLATION DETAILS

I-JOISTS
Squash blocks are required at bearing locations where concentrated loads from above must be transferred through the floor assembly. Blocks should be made of 2x4s or 2x6s, oriented vertically, and 1/16 in. longer than the depth of the joist.

Web stiffeners are required to provide a nailing surface when certain types of hangers are used. The web stiffener should be made

of either plywood or OSB sheathing or utility-grade spruce-pine-fir (SPF) lumber.

Blocking prevents joists from rolling, and transfers shear and vertical loads from above. Cutoffs from I-joists or structural rim boards can be used. Both APA-The Engineered Wood Association and the Wood I-Joist Manufacturers Association (WIJMA) recommend against using sawn lumber for blocking.

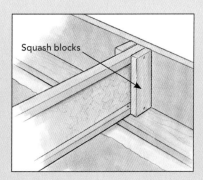

Squash blocks

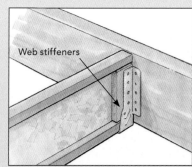

Web stiffeners

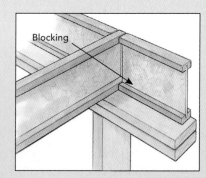

Blocking

peace of mind. "I want to hand my plans over to someone and get back my layout and design options," Guertin says. "I don't want to spend my time looking at span tables and punching numbers into a calculator in order to figure this out."

This level of customization is why it's difficult to say how much a floor truss will cost per lineal foot. Taft Ketchum from PDJ Components Inc. in Chester, N.Y., points out that truss sourcing varies by region, too, which makes it hard to gauge pricing. "In our area, lumberyards act as the middleman, but in other parts of the country, builders deal directly with the truss plant," he says.

It's interesting to note that unlike with dimensional lumber and I-joists, deeper doesn't necessarily mean more expensive. Ketchum explains that depending on the design, a 12-in.-deep truss might be more expensive than a 16-in.-deep truss simply because of the amount of material used. A shallower truss may call for more webs, which means more wood, more labor, and ultimately, higher cost.

The bottom line is that you'll pay more for trusses and I-joists than for dimensional lumber. You'll also get a more stable, sometimes fully customized product that's faster to install and easier on the subs.

FLOOR TRUSSES

Bottom chord-bearing trusses sit on top of a mudsill, beam, or bearing wall. The ends are typically tied together with a 2x "ribbon board," which provides lateral stability during installation. Structural wall sheathing is often used for lateral stability. Special blocking panels may be required to transfer shear loads through the assembly.

Top chord-bearing trusses are supported on the top of the mudsill, beam, or bearing wall by their top chords. They're used most often in applications that require the floor be close to grade level. They can't roll like bottom chord-bearing trusses, but they still require bracing before the subfloor is installed.

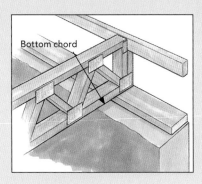

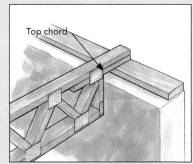

Building a Hybrid Timber-Frame Floor

BY SAM KOERBER

When I built my first house at the age of 19, I wanted it to be cheap but interesting. My dad suggested using doubled-up 2x10s for the floor joists, skinning them along the bottom edge with 1x4s to hide the seam, and capping them with tongue-and-groove planks. It amounted to a budget version of a real timber-frame floor, but it worked, and living in that house caused the look of exposed structural timbers to seep into my design psyche and become an essential part of my style.

It was only after building a few more houses with this technique that I realized my doubled joists weren't much cheaper than real timbers, and that

2x cleat

1

AdvanTech, with seams taped

4

1 BEAM IN WALL. If a beam lands in a pocket below the top plate of a wall—a common situation in 1½-story frames—it's helpful to notch the studs along that wall so that an inset 2x cleat can be added for nailing the tongue-and-groove subfloor planks.

2 BEAM ON TOP PLATE. As with other structural beams, timber beams landing on a stud wall must be supported by posts. But because timbers vary, it's often necessary to remove material from the bottom of a beam where it bears on the wall plate in order to keep the floor above level.

3 DOVETAILED MORTISES. To avoid visible fasteners, joists connect to beams with dovetailed tenons that fit into slightly oversize mortises. Hardwood shims are driven along each cheek of the loose-fitting tenons, drawing the pieces together.

4 PLANKS COMPLETE THE LOOK. A layer of tongue-and-groove planks installed over the joists and beams mimics traditional board sheathing, and a layer of AdvanTech subfloor with Zip System tape protects the installation from the weather until the house is dried in.

SEQUENCE FOR A SNUG FIT

To maximize efficiency, we cut as many joists as possible before anything is lifted into position. To do this, we mark beam positions on the subfloor and take measurements to create a joist cutlist. This floor breaks down into three sections, but only the two outer sections are cut ahead of time, leaving the center joists to be measured once the beams are set in place.

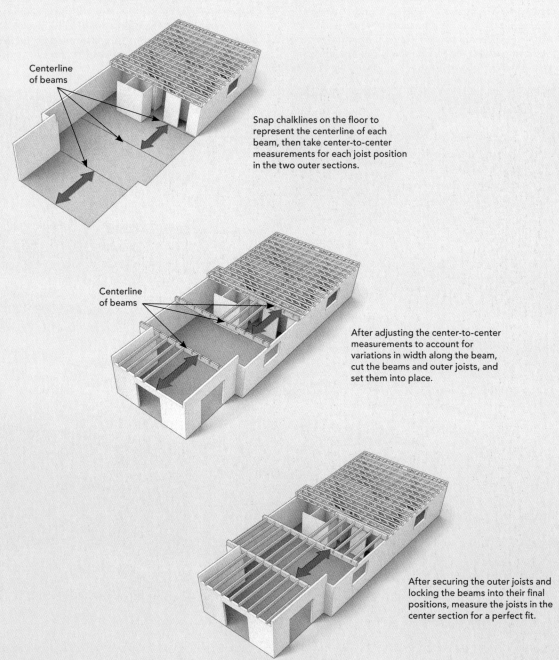

Centerline of beams

Snap chalklines on the floor to represent the centerline of each beam, then take center-to-center measurements for each joist position in the two outer sections.

Centerline of beams

After adjusting the center-to-center measurements to account for variations in width along the beam, cut the beams and outer joists, and set them into place.

After securing the outer joists and locking the beams into their final positions, measure the joists in the center section for a perfect fit.

although the look was OK, it still wasn't what I really wanted. I had seen other builders apply solid, nonstructural timbers to finished drywall ceilings, but that seemed way too much work for what, to me, wasn't authentic.

So when the next opportunity came along, I went with a hybrid approach that I still use today: a conventional stick-built house that incorporates real structural timbers and traditional joinery, completed mostly with common carpentry tools. This represents an authentic and sparing taste of the timber-frame aesthetic.

Timbers can mix with 2xs

My usual approach is to frame one part of the main-level ceiling in timbers and then use dimensional or engineered lumber elsewhere in the house. In order to make this work, the needs of each room must be coordinated with the realities of having exposed timbers, because you're surrendering the drywall-covered joist bays that are used to hide mechanicals. Upstairs bathrooms need to be located so that waste lines are not visible from below. Similarly, if you want recessed lighting in the kitchen, it makes more sense to finish this area with conventional drywall.

MORTISES FOR THE BEAMS. The beams are set atop timbers that span pairs of stout sawhorses 20 in. tall, which is a comfortable working height. This allows the beams to be rolled as necessary as mortises are roughed out on both sides.

KERFS ON A BEVEL. Working with two saws—one that bevels left and one that bevels right—a pair of carpenters can work their way quickly down the length of a beam, establishing the shape of each mortise.

CHISEL TO THE LINES. Although any wide chisel can get the job done, the extra length of a large timber-framing chisel makes it the ideal tool for removing the bulk of the kerfed waste.

A SQUARE SEAT. To ensure that the joists bear solidly on the bottom of each mortise without the need for tapered shims, check the bottom for square against the side of the beam.

 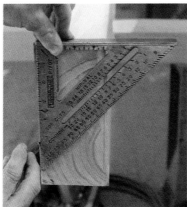 

MARK THE TENONS. Working from the center of the joist end, measure an equal distance to each side, then square down the height of the beam mortises. Connect the dots to mark the bottom of the tenon.

You also need to think about beam and joist spans, and about whether you want to (or can) get away without posts. In most cases, posts are necessary, and they can reinforce the timber-frame look. The clients for the house shown here wanted a clear-span look, so we eliminated posts by supporting the beams with a trusslike setup connected to the roof framing above. Whether or not posts are used, beams and joists should be sized by an architect or engineer.

When the plans are finalized, they become your cutlist for ordering the timbers from a sawyer. I typi-cally order posts and joists 1 ft. or 2 ft. longer than needed to allow enough room for the tenons to be cut, and I get a couple of extra joists in case I make a mistake during layout and assembly. For beams, I order only what I need, and I have them cut to exact length if possible.

Although I've used poplar and oak in previous timber-framing projects, my favorite wood is white pine. It's straight, has the lowest shrinkage ratio of any species, works easily with both power tools and hand tools, and looks beautiful when finished with either linseed oil or stain.

Fresh-cut, so-called green lumber is the norm in timber framing, but depending on the sawyer, it may be possible to pay extra to have the wood partially kiln dried. I use the word partially because I've found that even kiln-dried timbers still have a relatively high moisture content. So while they may be slightly lighter in weight, and joints may stay a little tighter because there's going to be a bit less shrinkage after installation, I don't bother paying the extra for kiln-dried timbers. It's best to go into this project with an understanding that no matter what you do, the timbers will be heavy, and they will shrink and move as they dry. That's where technique comes into play.

TENONS FOR THE JOISTS

DEPENDING ON THEIR POSITION IN THE LAYOUT, joists bear directly on a plate or connect to a beam with a dovetail tenon on each end, or they connect with a tenon on one end and a square cut on the other. The top of each joist needs to sit flush and square to the beams in order to adequately support the floor sheathing above, so the layout always references from the top face.

UP AND DOWN. Set the circular saw to a 15° bevel and a 2-in. depth of cut, then make a pair of cuts along the marked lines—down one side and then up the other—to shape the dovetailed sides of the tenon.

REMOVE THE WASTE. After scribing a line around the outside of the joist, cut away the waste to leave the finished tenon.

Framing for finish

Because this hybrid approach is essentially structural framing that doubles as finish carpentry, you need to think like both a framer and a finish carpenter. The most challenging parts of the job are strategiz-

ing, moving the material efficiently, and designing and executing the installation to take into account all the other parts of the house that will be built along with the floor. Because the framing will all be visible, you have to lay out and cut the various joints with care so that they result in a finished look.

All of the timber-frame joints I use have a functional purpose. The mortise-and-tenon joints used at post-and-beam connections keep the post in line with the beam even as both members shrink and twist. The dovetail tenon joints for the joists and the beam allow the top of the beam to be flush with the top of the joists, and the shims pull it tight to counteract some of the shrinkage that occurs as the pieces dry.

I've developed a workflow that allows me to cut all the necessary joints with common carpentry tools. In addition to the usual bevel-left and bevel-right 7¼-in. circular saws, power planer, and high-speed sander, I use a 2-in. timber-framing chisel, a wooden mallet, and a drawknife, which is great for dressing the edges of the timbers. You may find that a 10-in. or even 16-in. circular saw, a chain mortiser, and a wide beam planer such as the Makita KP312 are all helpful also.

Big-timber logistics

Being efficient in how you move the timbers is crucial. It's best to arrange the timber delivery when an excavator is on-site for backfilling and grading. The excavator can pick up the bundle with a couple of straps and then place it on the main floor. If the walls are up, I might work on the joists outside the house and then carry them in for installation. The beams are usually too heavy to carry easily, so if I can't have them dropped inside, I at least have them placed so that they lean into a doorway. This way, we can maneuver the beams into the house on rollers made from offcuts of PVC pipe and then lift them onto sawhorses one end at a time so that they can be worked more comfortably.

For working on the timbers, I like to have four 20-in.-tall pony-style sawhorses. I set them up in

DRESS, SAND, AND INSTALL

To give the timbers a hand-dressed look, we ease all the edges, do a rough sanding to remove any layout marks, and treat all cuts with a wax sealer such as Green Wood End Sealer ($16, rockler.com) before lifting each piece into place. A final sanding is usually necessary but will come after the wood has dried to a lower moisture content.

REMOVE THE CROWN. Snap a chalkline along one side of each timber (held down 1 in. from each end) so that any major deviation from the 1-in. benchmark can be shaved off with a power planer (right).

EASE THE EDGES. Holding it nearly flat, pull a sharp drawknife down the length of each timber to ease the edges and disguise imperfections.

ROUGH SANDING. Use a high-speed sander with 40-grit paper to clean up the rough-hewn results of the drawknife work and to remove layout marks.

SHIMS FOR THE TENONS. Untapered oak shims draw the shoulders of the joists tight against the beam face, locking the joists into place.

SCREWS FOR THE PLATES. With the drywall groove aligned to the interior face of the stud wall, a single structural screw (TimberLOKs were used here) driven through the top of its end secures the joist to the top plate below. Because the lumber is wet, no pilot hole is needed.

EASY LIFTING. A wheeled material lift, available from rental yards for about $60 a day, makes quick work of lifting the beams and joists into position.

pairs—ideally over a well-supported section of the subfloor framing—and set one of the timbers across each pair in order to give me a surface for stacking the rest of the pile. This setup allows several guys to be working on the timbers at the same time, and it provides room to roll the timbers as necessary.

To raise the finished pieces on this job, I rented a material lift for about $60 a day. The lift is rated at 750 lb. and is the perfect tool for lifting, maneuvering, and setting timbers from a subfloor deck. If there is a strong anchor point overhead—either part of the house frame or a temporary rig—a chain hoist also can be used.

We try to put up the timbers during a stint of dry weather, then we install the tongue-and-groove planks, followed by a layer of ¾-in. AdvanTech sheathing. If noise is a concern, we install a layer of ½-in. Homasote atop the tongue-and-groove planks and then add the sheathing. AdvanTech is not intended to be waterproof, but sealing the seams with Zip System tape goes a long way toward preventing water from seeping through during construction. This last detail protects the beams from water stains that develop from rain and snow that fall during construction, saving a lot of sanding in the end.

Installing a Subfloor

BY ANDY ENGEL

1 START STRAIGHT. Snap a chalkline across the joists 4 ft. from the outside of the rim joist.

2 START SPREADING THE GLUE. Apply a bead of adhesive on each joist up to the chalkline.

The subfloor is the layer of structural sheathing applied directly to the joists that provides a base for all the finish floors to come. Some types of flooring, such as carpet or traditional hardwood, can be installed directly on top of the subfloor. Others—such as tile, vinyl, and some engineered-wood products—require an additional layer called underlayment before they are installed.

The most important function of a subfloor is to create a structural diaphragm that helps to distribute wind and seismic loads through the house frame. That's the main reason subflooring has a code-specified nailing schedule (every 6 in. on edges parallel to joists and 12-in. spacing in the field). But perhaps the most obvious reason that proper sub-

floor installation is important is to minimize floor squeaks down the road. If subflooring panels can move against the joists or abutting sheets, they will squeak. Gluing the panels down in addition to nailing them is considered best practice for eliminating

3 LAY THE FIRST SHEET. Align the edge with the chalkline. Choose either the tongue or the edge of the sheet; just be consistent.

4 START AT ONE CORNER AND WORK OUT. Keep the nails between ⅜ in. and ½ in. from the edges of the panel.

5 SPACE THE NAILS CORRECTLY. Drive the nails no farther apart than 6 in. on the short edges and 12 in. in the middle of the sheet, completely nailing each sheet before moving to the next one.

squeaks, although it's not included in the structural calculations, nor is it required by code. Some engineered floor specifications, however, may require the use of adhesive. Whenever working with engineered floor systems, be sure to follow the manufacturer's instructions to the letter.

New materials solve old problems

Most subflooring used these days is either ¾-in. plywood or ¾-in. OSB, one long edge of which has a tongue and the other long edge a matching groove. Tongue-and-groove subflooring was pretty new to the market when I started framing in the 1980s. Prior to that, the standard was regular old ⅝-in. or ¾-in. CDX plywood. To support the edges of the sheets so that they didn't sag between the joists, carpenters installed blocking where the long edges of the sheets would meet. This required extra material for the blocking as well as a fair amount of extra work.

The introduction of tongue-and-groove subflooring eliminated the need for the extra work of installing the blocking because the sheets support each other when their edges interlock. Getting the sheets to go together could sometimes be challenging, however, particularly if they'd been exposed to much moisture prior to installation. The solution

6 SPACE THE ENDS OF SUBSEQUENT SHEETS. Use a 10d common nail to create an expansion space between sheets. After a few sheets, you may need to cut one shorter to keep the edges on the joists.

7 REPEAT THESE STEPS ON SUCCEEDING ROWS. Stagger the sheet ends, and slide their grooves over the tongues of the previous row.

8 TAP GENTLY. If the tongues and grooves in succeeding rows of sheathing don't engage easily, a few taps with a hammer against a 2x block should be enough to persuade them together.

with the commodity sheets I saw in years past was to beat them together with a sledgehammer, using a length of 2x to cushion the blows.

Even after subflooring has been installed, extended exposure to the elements often can lead to trouble. Plywood subflooring can delaminate, and OSB is famous for its edges swelling (sometimes to the point where the joints must be sanded down prior to the finish flooring being installed). The market responded to these problems with premium grades of subflooring, such as the Huber AdvanTech used here. The company promises that AdvanTech can be exposed to the weather for 500 days with no edge swelling severe enough to require sanding, and says that carpenters should never need to use more than a few taps with a block and a framing hammer to drive the sheets home.

THE RIGHT NAILS MATTER

USE RING-SHANK OR SCREW-SHANK nails long enough to penetrate the joists at least 1 in. Smooth-shank nails can withdraw over time.

SUBFLOOR ADHESIVES

ALTHOUGH NOT REQUIRED BY CODE, gluing down subflooring helps to prevent squeaks. That's so widely accepted that I've never seen a subfloor installed without adhesive.

The most common adhesives come in 28-oz. tubes and are applied using a large caulk gun. Keep these adhesives warm in the winter. When cold, they don't adhere as well, and they become extremely viscous. I've broken guns trying to get cold glue to come out. Also, pay attention to the expiration date. When the solvents in old glue evaporate, it thickens, is hard to apply, and doesn't adhere well.

More recently, polyurethane foam adhesives have hit the market, and they're applied with the same type of applicator gun used with pro-style cans of spray foam. With foam-based adhesives, the problem is more likely to be the glue hardening inside a gun that's unused for months. Unopened foam cans have a shelf life of 18 months.

Many adhesives have application temperature ranges, and some can be applied to wet or icy lumber while others should not be. Never put down more than a sheet's worth of adhesive at one time or it can skin over and lose adhesion. Also, walking on joists is dicey enough without adding slippery, wet adhesive to the equation.

Fast, Accurate Floor Sheathing

BY DANNY KELLY

As a carpenter turned general contractor, I'm always happy when we start installing the subfloor on the first level of a new house. Floor sheathing means that we can finally stop slogging around in the mud and will soon have a nice level surface for setting up tools and ladders. Sheathing a floor like the 1,800-sq.-ft. one shown here can take all day with an inexperienced crew, but the guys I work with were able to bang out this floor in a little under an hour.

On most houses, the longest exterior wall perpendicular to the floor joists is the place to start sheathing a floor. With a four-person crew, two carpenters move and cut panels, and two place and nail the sheets to the joists.

16 in. o.c.

19.2 in. o.c.

24 in. o.c.

LAY DOWN A WORKSURFACE

IT'S TOO DANGEROUS TO WALK ON THE TOPS OF JOISTS while sheathing a subfloor, so create a worksurface by covering the floor joists with as many sheets of tongue-and-groove sheathing as you need to move around safely. Arrange the panels so that all the tongues and all the grooves are oriented consistently. Start with a full sheet on the corner of the longest exterior wall perpendicular to the joists. The next row starts with a half-sheet. One pair of carpenters should keep laying and nailing down full sheets, while another pair stocks the floor with full sheets and cuts and places partial sheets. Alternate full sheets and half-sheets to start each row. Some sheathing has marks indicating common on-center spacings (photo, p. 107).

HOW TO PUT DOWN A SUBFLOOR FAST. Two carpenters move panels and make cuts while two position, glue, and nail the sheets. While one sheet is being nailed, another is dragged into place.

LINE IT UP. Line up the edge of one sheet with the previous sheet, making sure that all the tongues and all the grooves are facing the same direction. (The author's crew starts with a tongue toward the outside wall.) Don't drag the panels through the adhesive.

We cut the sheets to length after they've been nailed in place; this is faster and eliminates layout and measuring mistakes. We're careful to cut floor sheathing flush with the band joist. Otherwise, overhanging pieces will prevent the wall sheathing from fitting tight to the band joist. To get the sheets to fall on the center of the floor joists, subtract ¾ in. from the first joist cavity. Then the first sheet can start flush with the band joist without any waste.

LET IT GO. Drop the panel onto the joists as close to its final position as possible; otherwise, you'll mess up the subfloor adhesive when you slide the panel into place. It doesn't matter whether you drop the tongue or the groove edge.

TACK A CORNER. One carpenter moves the sheet so that its leading edge is lined up with the adjacent sheet. Then the nail-gun operator tacks the corner with a single nail. He pauses while his teammate moves the other end into position.

NAIL IT OFF. With the sheet in position, the nail-gun operator drives a nail or two to lock the sheet in its final position and then nails the rest of the sheet. With an experienced team, positioning and tacking take seconds. Panels overhanging the edge of the band joist will be cut in place later.

MEASURE FROM UNDERNEATH; SNAP LINES ON TOP. Feed a tape measure under the panel until it hits the band joist. Transfer the measurement to the top of the panel, and snap chalklines to guide a circular saw. Set the blade so that it just cuts through the subfloor and doesn't damage the band joist.

PUT OFF CUTTING WHEN YOU CAN. When possible, save the job of cutting unusually sized panels like the ones around this crawlspace opening until you've finished laying all the sheets. Cutting odd-shaped panels is a good job for less experienced carpenters while the more senior carpenters move on to snapping lines and laying out plates for wall framing.

RUN WILD! Save time, and eliminate layout and measuring mistakes by cutting odd-shaped panels in place. The first piece in a row will be a full sheet or a half-sheet, but the last piece at the opposite end likely will be an odd-width offcut.

DO USE A SLEDGE SPARINGLY. The tongues and grooves on subflooring are designed to gap panels properly, so the panels shouldn't be beaten together except when the tongue has been damaged by rough handling. When that's the case, use a sledgehammer to get the sheets to meet up. A board prevents the hammer face from doing additional damage.

DON'T MESS UP THE GLUE. To prevent smearing the subfloor adhesive, stand the sheet on edge in the proper spot, and let it drop into the glue. A well-timed pull with the ball of your foot can help to keep the panel edge close to the previous row.

DO CHECK THE JOIST SPACING. Warped joists don't necessarily line up with on-center spacing, so check the spacing before nailing, then use a hammer to coax joists into the proper position. Subflooring with spacing marks saves time.

DON'T LET THE GLUE DRY. Apply only as much glue as can be covered with sheathing quickly. Save time by cutting the plastic nozzles on the glue tubes all at once. (An inner seal keeps the opened tubes from drying.) Water-based adhesives, which are more environmentally friendly, work better than they used to, but solvent-based adhesives are still more forgiving in wet weather.

DO USE ENOUGH NAILS. Nail subfloor panels every 12 in. in the field and every 6 in. along panel edges. Keep fasteners ³/₈ in. from panel edges for maximum hold. For ¾-in.-thick sheets, use 8d (2½ in.) common nails or gun nails approved by local code. The author uses ring-shank nails and adds screws once the house is dried in.

THE FLOOR ISN'T SQUARE. NOW WHAT?

MY CREW AND I RECENTLY REFRAMED the interior of a 100-year-old brownstone building on Beacon Hill in Boston. The building was so out of square that it was like building in a carnival funhouse. We found that as long as the joists were parallel with one another, installing the subfloor could proceed as normal.

We snapped a line perpendicular to the joists 48 in. from the band joist. The first and last rows were tapered rips, and the first and last pieces in a row were angled. All the field pieces were full, uncut sheets.
—*Brian McCarthy, owner of McCarthy General Contracting in Stow, Mass.*

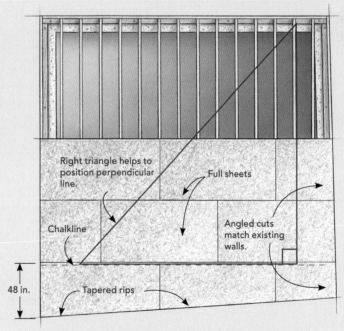

Right triangle helps to position perpendicular line.

Full sheets

Chalkline

Angled cuts match existing walls.

48 in.

Tapered rips

A right triangle is used to create a reference line perpendicular to the floor joists. The line should be 48 in. wide at its widest point to match the panel width.

Wall Framing

BY ROB MUNACH

When constructed correctly, a house's frame resists a variety of building loads, such as wind and snow. When built poorly, the frame will fail. When overbuilt, it can lead to energy losses through thermal bridging.

To be a successful framer, you should have a comprehensive understanding of wall assemblies and employ advanced-framing techniques—including those illustrated here—when appropriate. Keep in mind that while advanced framing reduces energy losses, resource consumption, and construc-

tion costs by using significantly less lumber than the typically framed house, it lacks the redundancy to stand up to extreme loads like a falling tree. So use advanced-framing techniques sensibly.

By looking at the components of a wall assembly and the role each component plays within a wall, you can begin to understand how a wall functions as a system. That's critical information, whether you're following standard building practices or advanced techniques. Turn the page to see how it works.

WALL FRAMING

HEADERS transfer wind-uplift loads and dead loads around openings in a wall assembly. They also transfer wind loads that blow on the face of the wall into the king studs. If exterior walls are not load bearing, headers can be constructed similar to the sill using a stud on the flat. In this case, a header has to resist wind loads blowing only on the face of the wall.

Installed on the flat, the **SILL PLATE** supports the window and transfers wind loads blowing on the face of the wall into the king studs. In a lot of cases, only a single sill plate is needed, not a double. Multiple sill plates are sometimes needed in wide openings.

Spaced 24 in. o.c., 2x6 **STUDS** carry the downward load of the rafters, joists, or top plates above them. The studs in a wall also resist wind blowing against the wall and wind-uplift loads in walls that are not fully sheathed with plywood or OSB. This wall assembly yields more space for insulation than a wall with 2x4s spaced 16 in. o.c.

FLOOR JOISTS resist live and dead loads. When joined with the rim joist, they create a system that resists racking forces on the house.

CRIPPLES are short 2x blocks above and below rough openings. Those above the header transfer wind and gravity loads from the top plate to the header. They also give you something to nail sheathing to. The cripples below a sill serve mostly as nailers for the sheathing, so the number that you use can be reduced to only one in most instances.

The **TOP PLATES** carry the downward load from the roof rafters or floor joists above. They also act as a "shear collector" by distributing shear loads from the floor or roof assembly above and transferring them along the length of the wall to sheathed corners or braced wall segments. When the rafters or joists are directly in line with the studs of the wall below, only a single top plate is needed. Double top plates, however, add strength and redundancy to the structure and may be required in high-wind and seismic areas.

HEADER HANGERS support the weight of the header and transfer its gravitational load into the king studs. They replace jack studs.

OSB or plywood **SHEATHING** on the exterior of the wall resists uplift on the top plate and, as a shear-resisting element, keeps the wall from racking. In some cases, the midwall sheathing is replaced with nonstructural rigid-foam insulation. The corners of the house are then reinforced with plywood or fabricated shear walls.

Load path highlighted in red

KING STUDS prevent the header from rotating within the assembly and transfer wind and dead loads to the roof framing above or floor framing below.

The **MUDSILL** is a rotproof member that attaches the frame to the foundation.

The **RIM JOIST** transfers loads from the bottom of one wall to the top of a lower wall, or from the bottom of a first-floor wall to the foundation. The rim joist also keeps the end of the floor joists from racking and transfers shear loads from the floor framing to the top plates or to the foundation wall. If properly designed, the rim joist also can act as the window and door header for the wall below. This is usually done only with smaller openings. Care should be exercised to ensure that splices in the rim joist do not end up over these openings.

Fast and Accurate Wall Framing

BY MIKE NORTON

I f there's a glamorous job in carpentry, it's not framing. It might be finish work; everything looks so good after that final piece of molding is nailed in place and the job is complete. Framing, on the other hand, is called "rough," and it requires an experienced imagination to see the finished product in its earliest stage. But framing embodies the physics of the structure, and if you don't get it right, the house will fail. You'll also have a hard time nailing your fancy trim where there is no blocking.

Whether the plans call for traditional stick framing or optimum-value engineering, the skills are relatively simple: straight and square cuts, a good hammer technique, economy of motion, and a strong back. There are a few tricks, however, that make the job easier and the results more professional. Here, I'll explain some of the methods I've picked up, using a simple exterior wall as an example.

Layout is critical

Even though you're probably the one who laid the sill plates and framed the deck, it's still a good idea to make sure that the deck is square before framing the walls. The simplest method to use is to check the corners by measuring a 3/4/5 triangle and then extending the angle with a reference chalkline. I've

GET SQUARE AND PARALLEL WALLS WITH A LASER. A key step in laying out walls is to establish square corners and parallel walls, a task streamlined with the use of a laser. Once square corners have been set, the plate layout lines can be snapped.

VERIFY THE 90. A check of the target placed on the opposite corner verifies the 90° angle generated by the laser. Adjust the plate location if the original mark doesn't match the target.

A GOOD LASER MAKES LAYOUT FASTER AND MORE ACCURATE. The author uses a laser that fires a constant beam in five directions that is visible in daylight (Pacific Laser Systems; PLS-5 kit). The first step is to mark the plate width in all corners, set the laser, and aim it toward the first target.

HIT THE BULL'S-EYE. Placed on the next corner over the plate mark, the target indicates when the laser is lined up.

ESTABLISH PARALLEL LINES. From the corners verified by the laser, measure and mark the opposite wall-plate positions (4). Snap layout chalklines for the plates (5).

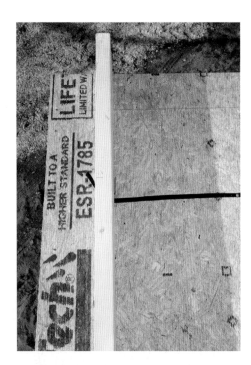

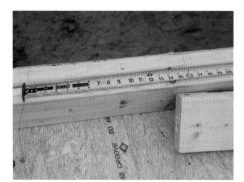

NO MATH, JUST MARK. When laying out a plate, it's faster to mark the edge of the first stud, drive a nail into the first mark, and then pull 16-in. intervals from there.

LAY OUT THE PLATES ONCE. It's usually easiest to build walls on the deck and then lift them into place. The first step is to mark out stud, window, and door openings on the plates. A length of metal packing strap nailed to the plate and deck is good insurance against a wall dropping off the deck's edge as it's raised.

EFFICIENT LAYOUT. For a quick layout, place the top plate behind the bottom plate, and mark both at the same time. This temporary placement also keeps deck clutter to a minimum.

TOE THE PLATE. Lay the bottom plate on edge, and align it with the chalkline. Toenail it to the deck, nailing every 2 ft. or so. Once the wall is built, the completed structure is anchored to the deck and is less likely to move as it's raised.

found it faster, however, to use a laser that shoots two lines at 90°. Two people can square up a deck in about 10 minutes, and there's less chance for error. If the deck isn't square, it's usually within a ¼-in. tolerance that we can correct by moving the plate location marks out beyond the deck edge or inward toward the center of the deck.

After squaring up the deck, we snap lines for the plates. While we're at it, we also snap a reference centerline across the deck so that we can check that walls are parallel or, when it's snapped to represent the ridgeline, use it to lay out a gable wall.

We frame the walls flat on the deck by first toe-nailing the bottom plates down on edge along the chalklines. After double-checking the window and door schedule, we mark these locations on the plates. I also figure out where the partitions intersect the wall and mark the location of the backers. If there's a conflict between the partition's placement and the eventual locations of interior trim, I usually call the architect before making the necessary adjustments.

Framing layout is a critical part of the process, so I always double-check my measurements. I cut the bottom plate to length first, then the top plates. I usually wait to install the second top plate until adjoining walls are raised so that the plate ties the walls together.

With the bottom and top plates placed together temporarily, I start marking the layout from the left and go right. After I mark the first stud on the bottom plate, I drive a nail at the line and pull 16 in. from there, marking the X beyond the line that indicates the stud location. At the same time, I transfer the layout to the top plate.

If I have a straight wall and a simple floor frame above, I mark the floor-joist layout onto the second top plate's face so that we don't have to do it after we lift the wall.

AN ORGANIZED LIST. After assigning each window a letter designation and listing the parts' measurements, cut and stack the parts in discrete piles.

PRODUCTION-STYLE ASSEMBLY. Assigning one carpenter the task of cutting parts at the chopsaw station means that the rest of the crew can keep nailing. If there are a number of identical windows, it's faster for the cut man to make parts and assemble the windows as units.

ALWAYS CHECK FOR SQUARE. After the wall has been nailed together, measure both diagonals to make sure the wall is square before starting to sheathe.

EASIER ON THE GROUND. It's safer, faster, and neater to cut out the window openings with a circular saw as the sheathing is installed.

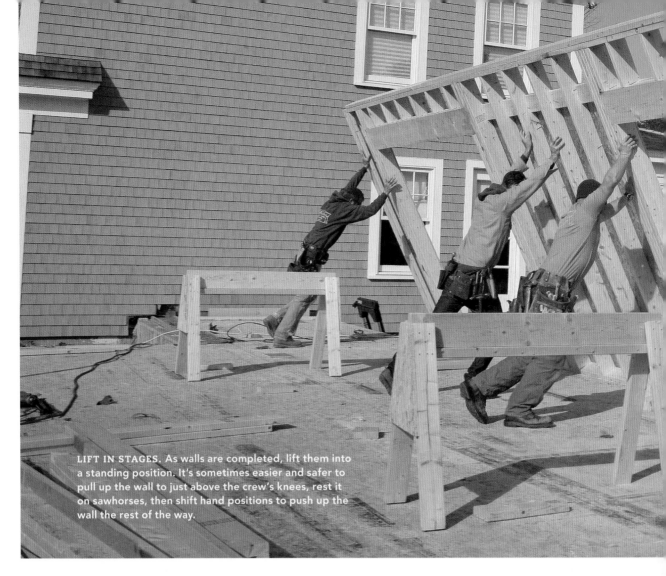

LIFT IN STAGES. As walls are completed, lift them into a standing position. It's sometimes easier and safer to pull up the wall to just above the crew's knees, rest it on sawhorses, then shift hand positions to push up the wall the rest of the way.

1 SET THE SPRINGBOARDS TO BRACE THE WALL TEMPORARILY. With the wall braced, start the straightening process by nailing one end of a pine 1x8 to the underside of the top plate or to a header.

2 TACK THE BOTTOM. While one carpenter pushes down on the board, the other checks the string with a 2x gauge. The trick is to increase the tension by overbending the board so that it pulls the wall into the string. The first carpenter then tacks the springboard end to the deck and releases the tension on the board.

3 PULL THE WALL. One carpenter pushes a shorter leg into the underside of the springboard, bringing the top plate back toward the string. When the gauge indicates that the top plate is straight, the other carpenter nails the leg to the springboard, locking it and the wall into place.

Cutting duplicate components all at once is faster

I've found that it's more efficient to have one of the crew designated as the cut man at a chopsaw. (Mounted on a stand with adjustable stops, the saw makes production work simple and accurate.) Wall studs, headers, window and door parts, and other duplicates all get cut there.

If the house has many of the same windows, I put together a cut list so that we can cut the legs below the window and the cripples above at the same time as the headers and sills. On the list, I group the windows with the same header length so that the cut man can cut everything without having to adjust his jig.

It's usually easier for the cut man to cut and assemble the headers, jacks, sills, legs, and other pieces into door and window units that we then can incorporate into the frame. If they're all various sizes, we assemble the doors or the windows as part of the wall. When the houses are fairly complicated and have different wall heights and large windows of different sizes, I have someone ready on the deck to cut all the legs and cripples as we frame the wall. Because the width of the header stock can vary by ¼ in. from one 2x10 to another, most times we cut the cripples to length, install them, and then cut the jacks to the corresponding length. The rough opening's height may decrease by a fraction of an inch, but as long as the window fits in the rough opening, it's OK.

Sheathing layout is important

Once we've assembled a wall on the deck and measured its diagonals to make sure it's square, we begin sheathing. We pay careful attention to the engineer's plans, including the nailing pattern on the sheathing and the location of vertical sheets of plywood to hold down the corners of the house. If a wall is over a certain height or the engineer requires longer sheets for a hold-down, we install blocking across the wall at the point where the seams meet.

We often use 4x8 plywood sheets to span from the mudsill to about a foot under the top plate of the wall. We then can use 4x10 sheets to span from that point to the second top plate of the second-floor wall. We also cut out windows and doors as we sheathe the walls, rather than doing so after we stand them up. It's safer, faster, and more precise.

Bracing and straightening

After we've raised a wall, we nail the plates to the deck and temporarily brace the wall with 2x6s so that it's pushed outward slightly. This makes it easier to raise an adjacent wall; it's also easier to pull the wall straight than to push it.

To straighten the walls, we nail a 2x block to each end of a wall at the top plate, then run a taut line between the two. Next, we install roughsawn 1x8 springboards at 8-ft. intervals. We cut them to length so they can span a 45° angle from the top plate to the deck, then we nail one end to the underside of the top plate. While one person checks the string with a 2x block, another flexes the board downward and tacks the lower end to the deck.

We jam a short length of board between the deck and the middle of the springboard and push it away from the wall until the gauge block shows that the wall is straight. Then we tack the short board to the springboard and the deck, locking the wall in.

USE THIS FOOLPROOF NONSLIP knot to stretch the stringline taut when straightening walls.

Pull the string tight, make a loop around your finger, and twist it (left).

Anchor the loop on the lower nail, and pull up on the string (bottom left).

While keeping tension on the string, pull down hard to compress the wraps on the loop (bottom right). Loosen the tension on the string, and the knot comes undone.

Framing a Gable Wall

BY BRIAN VOGT

After almost 20 years in the field, I know well that there are usually several good ways to complete any carpentry task. But here at North Bennet Street School (nbss.edu), where I now spend my days teaching carpentry, we stress fundamental textbook methods that minimize complex math and avoid specialty tools.

Our 2016 graduating class included 21 students, and, as we do every year, we used real construction projects to teach them carpentry. In addition to the small structures we built in our Boston shop at the beginning of the program, we finished with a full build. This year we framed a 24-ft. by 48-ft. barn and used the opportunity to take the students through the basics of building a gable wall: laying it out full scale on the attic floor, framing it, sheathing it, attaching the overhangs, and, finally, raising it safely.

Start with a full-scale layout

First, find the center of the building and snap a line parallel to the eaves. This represents the roof ridge.

If the roof will rest on kneewalls, add their height on both sides of the gable and snap a line in between.

Now use a construction calculator (or web application) to determine the theoretical ridge height:

- Enter RUN in feet and inches.
- Enter PITCH in inches (found on building plans).
- Press RISE.

Measure the height of the bird's-mouth plumb cut and subtract this amount from the overall depth of the rafter to find the height above plate (HAP). Add this HAP number to both the ridge height and kneewall height, and snap a line on the subfloor between them to mark the position of the rafter's top edge.

TRANSFER THE STUD LAYOUT

A FRAMING SQUARE WITH A STRAIGHT board clamped to it at the 10-in-12 roof pitch is used to lay out the studs on the rafter. The stud is marked along the vertical leg, and the 16-in. spacing is marked on the horizontal leg. The square is moved along the rafter and aligned with each tick mark, and the process repeated. The studs will be notched to fit around the rafter, and blocks of the same thickness as the notched studs hold rafters off the deck to allow the studs to slide under the rafter. L-shaped blocks set along the snapped chalkline keep the rafters in the correct location during framing.

FULL-SCALE LAYOUT

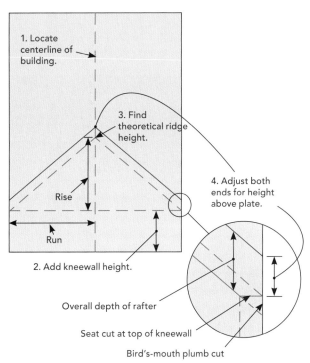

1. Locate centerline of building.

3. Find theoretical ridge height.

4. Adjust both ends for height above plate.

Rise

Run

2. Add kneewall height.

Overall depth of rafter

Seat cut at top of kneewall

Bird's-mouth plumb cut

Assembly-line cutting saves time

The tops of the gable studs must be cut to support the rafters. Marking and cutting the parts all at once minimizes setup and saw adjustments, saving time.

An angled cut at the top of each gable stud supports the rafter. These cuts are made by clamping several studs together and marking the roof pitch across them. Set the saw to cut 1½ in. deep, the thickness of the 2x rafter [1]. The tops of the studs extend to about 1 in. below the rafter's top edge. With the angled top cuts made, mark the vertical cheek cuts 1½ in. from the edge. Draw the line on all the studs using a combination square and a pencil [2]. Using a circular saw, make the cheek cuts, stopping at the top cuts you've already made. A finger on the saw's base guides the rip and keeps the blade parallel to the stud's edge [3]. Because the sawblade is round, a small part of the cheek cut must be completed with a handsaw. You could overcut with the circular saw, but finishing by hand takes seconds and the final result looks more professional [4].

With the top already notched, the studs are individually measured and cut [5]. The measurement is taken from the long side of the angled top cut to the plate. Measuring from the long side allows you to hook the tape for more-accurate measuring.

Door and window locations are marked on the plates during layout. Once the rest of the studs are nailed in place, giving the wall some rigidity, frame the openings, starting with the sills and jack studs [6, p. 128]. Once the jack studs are in place, position the header on top of them and fasten the king studs in place using pairs of nails spaced 16 in. o.c. [7]. The extra king stud the students are placing on this setup maintains the 16-in. o.c. spacing. Once the rest of the wall is framed, measure, cut, and nail cripples in place above rough openings. [8]

1 Gang-cut the tops.

2 Mark the cheeks.

3 Make stopped rips.

4 Finish the cuts.

5 Cut studs to length.

6 Start rough openings with jacks and sills.

7 Add headers and king studs.

8 Cripples come last.

Sheathe the wall on the deck

Sheathing and installing overhangs while the wall is lying flat is safer than working from a scaffold or ladder, but a word of caution: You will need wall jacks, machinery, or plenty of help to lift a wall this size.

Run the sheathing so it overhangs the bottom plate at least 12 in., so the wall will be fully connected to the floor system below [1]. In this engineered assembly, the sheathing was nailed to the studs with 8d nails spaced every 4 in. at panel edges and every 8 in. in the field. To save time and make fewer cuts, sheathe over window and door openings and cut them out in a clockwise direction with a heavy-duty router and a ½-in. bottom-bearing bit [2]. Use a router to cut off any overhanging sheathing, this time cutting counterclockwise (up the right side of the gable, then down the left) [3].

1 Start the sheathing in a corner.

2 Cover openings, then cut.

3 Cut overhanging sheathing.

4 Build overhangs on the bench.

5 Install overhangs on the deck.

It's easier to build the gable overhangs on a set of sawhorses. Bar clamps hold the parts together while they're fastened with 3-in. construction screws. [4] Starting from the top of the wall, align the overhangs so they're flush with the tops of the rafters and secure them with pairs of screws driven into each stud. [5]

Lift the wall enough to get a sturdy sawhorse underneath [6]. This divides the lift into two parts and allows an upright body position for the hardest part

of the lift, reducing the chance of back injury. Many helping hands and a pair of 2x6s attached to the gable studs with single structural screws that allow them to pivot help raise the wall [7]. Steel strapping keeps the bottom plate from slipping off the deck. Tag lines with floor-mounted anchors prevent the wall from falling. Once the wall is braced plumb, nail every 8 in. through the bottom plate into the band joist below [8].

6 Lift and pause.

7 Go all the way.

8 Nail it off.

Installing a Big Beam

BY ANDY ENGEL

Remodeling carpenters routinely set large beams in cases such as the one shown here, where the beam replaces a bearing wall. Whether a beam is made from engineered lumber or regular old 2x12s, the challenge is weight. Here, a new beam was made from three 16-ft.-long 1¾-in. by 11⅞-in. LVLs. It would have been difficult to raise the assembled beam, but the trick is to raise one piece at a time and then fasten the three together in place.

Replacing a wall with a beam requires carrying the loads while the old wall is being removed and the new beam is being installed. I built a temporary wall about 1 ft. beyond the old wall before removing it. I was lucky in that the joists above overlapped by several feet and so the temporary wall could be held back that far, which provided more room to work. In most cases, a temporary wall has to be built much closer to the existing wall, or even in contact with it, to catch the joist overlap and to support the floor.

This beam was engineered for its loads. (Lumberyards often provide this service for free.) Each end of the beam imposes a substantial load that requires a direct path through the framing to the foundation. Here, one end of the beam landed above the founda-

1 INSTALL KINGS AND PLATES. King studs tie the beam ends to the existing framing. Cut a new bottom plate long so that fasteners don't split it, screwing it to the framing below where the king and jack studs will go. Cut the plate flush to the jack studs later.

2 MARK THE BEAM LOCATION. To keep the beam straight, snap a chalkline on the joists between the edges of the king studs for a guide.

4 INSTALL JACK STUDS AND STOP BLOCKS. Two jacks were required at each end, but only one was installed at first to ease setting the beam. Temporary blocks on the jacks guide the beam placement.

tion wall, while the other was directly over a column in the basement. To complete the load path, all I had to do was place squash blocks (double or triple studs cut to the depth of the floor joists) between the bottom of the subfloor and the main beam below. In other cases, I might have had to add new columns and footings to carry the newly concentrated loads.

3 USE THE BEAM DEPTH TO SIZE THE JACKS. Measure the depth of the beam stock, and mark that on the king studs. Measure up to the mark from the bottom plate to determine the height of the jacks.

5 MEASURE THE BEAM LENGTH. Pull a tape between the king studs to determine the beam length. Deduct ¼ in. from that number so the beam members don't bind while being installed.

6 SLIP THE PLIES INTO PLACE. With the top leaning in, place both ends of the first ply at once onto the jack studs. A few sledgehammer taps along the bottom face stand the ply up.

7 INSTALL THE REMAINING PLIES LIKE THE FIRST. Nails can be used to join the plies, but structural screws set with an impact driver are better at drawing them into full contact with one another. Follow the designer's fastening schedule.

8 FASTEN TO THE JOISTS. Join each joist to the beam with a 3½-in. #10 multipurpose screw driven at an angle. In some circumstances, framing hardware is required to resist seismic or uplift loads.

9 A WIDE OPENING. With the second jack studs placed, the bottom plates trimmed, the squash blocks placed below, and the temporary wall removed, the new beam is ready for drywall.

USE THE RIGHT HARDWARE

Hurricane tie

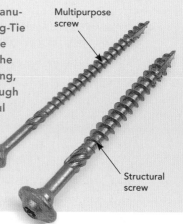

Multipurpose screw

Structural screw

IN COMBINATION WITH AN IMPACT DRIVER, structural screws by manufacturers such as FastenMaster, GRK, Screw Products, and Simpson Strong-Tie are increasingly used in place of nails and lag bolts. Although they're more expensive than those options, structural screws have some advantages. The GRK RSS screws used here require no pilot holes to minimize wood splitting, and they are configured to draw layers together as they are driven. Although multipurpose screws are not as strong as structural screws, they are useful for toe-screwed connections and temporary assemblies.

In areas where seismic and wind-uplift forces are big concerns, specific hardware such as hurricane ties are required to connect the beam to the rest of the framing.

The Right Header for Every Wall

BY MIKE GUERTIN

When I started framing houses in the late 1970s, the standard header for almost any size window and door opening was a double 2x12 with a ½-in. plywood spacer to bring the header flush with the stud edges in a 2x4 wall. When the header is pushed hard to the double top plate of an 8-ft.-high wall, its bottom sets up window and door head jambs 6 ft. 10 in. off the floor, perfect for standard 6-ft. 8-in. doors.

When high-performance homes gained market share in the late 1980s, the building industry looked for options to reduce the amount of lumber used to build headers—or to eliminate conventional headers altogether—in order to save resources, minimize thermal bridging, and provide more space for insulation. Double 2x12 headers are often oversize for the load, but they're still the standard. In most cases, there is no structural advantage to installing headers that are larger than required, and there are downsides. Not only do they cost more than right-size headers, but the deeper a lumber header is, the more likely it is to lead to drywall cracks as green lumber dries or dried lumber expands during seasonal humidity changes.

When I look at the prescriptive options available in the IRC, I'm surprised by how many builders still frame the way I did nearly 40 years ago. I guess bigger and beefier looks stronger and impresses clients, and I admit that it's easier to use the same-size headers throughout a house whether for a large patio door or a narrow window. Thoughtful header design takes planning and organization, but it's a better way to build. Shallower headers, single-ply headers, engineered lumber, innovative use of rim joists, and even no headers at all save material, money, and energy.

Right-size headers optimize lumber usage

Sizing a header for the load it will carry is pretty simple, can be done without an engineer, and usually results in headers that use less material. For conventionally framed houses, tables in the IRC help you determine the right-size header for the opening width and the load it supports (see the table on p. 138). In the 2012 IRC and earlier versions, the header span table for exterior bearing walls (R502.6[1]) was published in chapter 5, "Floors"—hardly a logical spot—and the table only included two-ply, three-ply, and four-ply headers. The 2012 IRC added a table for single-ply headers in chapter 6. The 2015 IRC consolidated this information in a single exterior-wall-header table (R602.7[1]) in chapter 6. This section includes similar tables for headers in interior walls and porches.

In addition to their listing in the table, single-ply headers have a subsection requiring that one 2x flat board be installed at the bottom of the header and another one on the top (unless the header is tight to the top plate).

The header options are listed by the number of plies (one to four) and the lumber size (2x4 to 2x12).

DO YOU EVEN NEED A HEADER?

The 2015 IRC says, "Load-bearing headers are not required in interior or exterior nonbearing walls. A single flat 2-in. by 4-in. member may be used...for openings up to 8 ft. in width" (R602.7.4).

In essence, the code doesn't require a header unless the end of a floor joist, roof rafter, or truss lands on that wall or there's a concentrated load bearing over the opening. You don't even need to install structural jack studs, since there is no load for them to bear.

A header also isn't required when a window or door is narrow enough to fit between studs on layout. This is more typical with framing on 24-in. centers. Then, when a window is less than 22 in. wide, you don't need a header; you just install 2x head and sill boards to box out the rough opening.

When an opening less than 8 ft. wide is in a nonbearing wall, a flat 2x does the job.

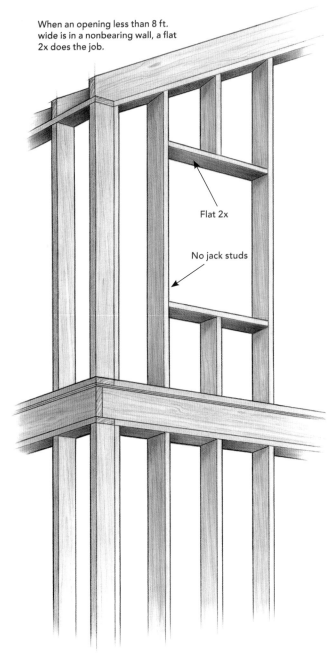

Flat 2x

No jack studs

While only three building widths (20 ft., 28 ft., and 36 ft.) are shown, the code permits you to interpolate for building widths between those listed. If you don't want to interpolate, you can just use the spans listed for the next-larger building width. Also in the tables are columns labeled NJ, meaning "number of jack studs" required under each end of the header.

Example: Find a header for an opening in an exterior wall on the first floor of a two-story house with a center-bearing wall. The house is 28 ft. wide, the rough-opening width is 3 ft. 2 in., and the snow load is 30 lb. per sq. ft. or less (found in IRC chapter 3).

1. Locate the group in the left column of the table on p. 138 that matches the situation.

2. Find the applicable snow load in the upper row.

3. Below the snow load, choose the building width.

4. Below the building width, look in the span column and find at least one span that matches or exceeds your opening (3 ft. 2 in. or greater). The closest in this case is 3 ft. 5 in.

5. Move directly left from the chosen span to the size column to find a header configuration. Use any header design for openings equal to or greater than yours. For spans up to 3 ft. 5 in., you can use a single 2x8 or two 2x6s, which could span up to 4 ft.

INTERPOLATION

If the house width falls between the three provided in the IRC, header spans can be interpolated with some simple math. For example, let's use the same rough opening and house configuration as before, except that in this case the house is 26 ft. wide. We'll use a single 2x8 header.

Begin with the difference in span for a given header configuration between the building width on each side of the actual building width. At 20 ft., a single 2x8 can span 3 ft. 11 in. At 28 ft., it can span 3 ft. 5 in., so the header span difference is 6 in. over 8 ft. To find the difference per foot, divide 6 in. by 8 ft.:

$$6 \text{ in.} \div 8 \text{ ft.} = 0.75 \text{ in. per ft.}$$

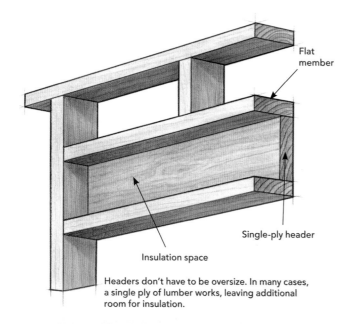

Headers don't have to be oversize. In many cases, a single ply of lumber works, leaving additional room for insulation.

Flat member

Single-ply header

Insulation space

Since the 26-ft.-wide building is 6 ft. wider than the 20-ft. width from the table, calculate the following:

0.75 in. per ft. × 6 ft. = 4.5 in.

Subtract the above number from the header span for a 20-ft.-wide building to find the allowable header span for a 26-ft.-wide building:

3 ft. 11 in. – 4.5 in. = 3 ft. 6.5 in.

Rim-board headers use existing framing

Why does a header have to be framed into an exterior wall when there's already a rim board in the floor framing above the top plate? A rim board often can bridge a window or door opening, and as of the 2015 IRC, there is a subsection on them (R602.7.2). Rim-board headers are sized according to the same table used to size regular headers, and in many cases the single-ply rim board you're already installing may eliminate the need for a conventional header below. In situations where the loads are greater or the opening is larger, the rim board can be sistered with additional material (photo at left). In all cases, there can be no joints in a rim-board header over the opening and for 6 in. past the outer bearing studs. The number of outer studs framing each end of the

GIRDER SPANS AND HEADER SPANS FOR EXTERIOR WALLS
(Maximum spans for Douglas fir–larch, hem-fir, southern pine, and spruce-pine-fir, and required number of jack studs)

Girders and headers supporting	Size	Ground snow load (lb. per sq. ft.)																
		30						50						70				
		Building width (ft.)																
		20		28		36		20		28		36		20		28		36
		Span	NJ	Span	NJ	Span	NJ	Span	NJ	Span	NJ	Span	NJ	Span	NJ	Span	NJ	Span	NJ
Roof, ceiling, and one center-bearing floor	1-2x8	3-11	1	3-5	1	3-0	1	3-7	1	3-0	2	2-8	2	-	-	-	-	-	-
	1-2x10	5-0	2	4-4	2	3-10	2	4-6	2	3-11	2	3-4	2	-	-	-	-	-	-
	1-2x12	5-10	2	4-9	2	4-2	2	5-5	2	4-2	2	3-4	2	-	-	-	-	-	-
	2-2x4	3-1	1	2-9	1	2-5	1	2-9	1	2-5	1	2-2	1	2-7	1	2-3	1	2-0	1
	2-2x6	4-6	1	4-0	1	3-7	2	4-1	1	3-7	2	3-3	2	3-9	2	3-3	2	2-11	2
	2-2x8	5-9	2	5-0	2	4-6	2	5-2	2	4-6	2	4-1	2	4-9	2	4-2	2	3-9	2
	2-2x10	7-0	2	6-2	2	5-6	2	6-4	2	5-6	2	5-0	2	5-9	2	5-1	2	4-7	3
	2-2x12	8-1	2	7-1	2	6-5	2	7-4	2	6-5	2	5-9	3	6-8	2	5-10	3	5-3	3
	3-2x8	7-2	1	6-3	2	5-8	2	6-5	2	5-8	2	5-1	2	5-11	2	5-2	2	4-8	2

rough opening must at least equal half the studs displaced by the opening, assuming you are using the maximum stud spacing permitted in table R602.3(5). This may sound confusing, but it's easy in practice. If there would be two studs falling in the opening, then you would need one jack stud at the left side of the opening and another at the right side.

According to the IRC, as long as floor joists have at least 1½ in. of top plate to bear on (say, a single rim board on a 2x4 top plate), hangers are not required. This is one case when I go beyond the code; I install hangers on all rim-board headers (see the drawing on p. 140).

Box headers take advantage of the sheathing

Box headers are made by installing structural-sheathing panels to the outside face or to the inside and outside faces of the framing between the top plate and a flat 2x at the head of a rough opening (see the drawing on p. 141). The sheathing and framing combine to act as a truss. Because they are built with a minimal amount of lumber, there is more space to fill with insulation. Box headers can be used only in walls supporting just a roof and a ceiling, and in walls supporting a roof, a ceiling, and one center-bearing floor with an interior center-bearing wall.

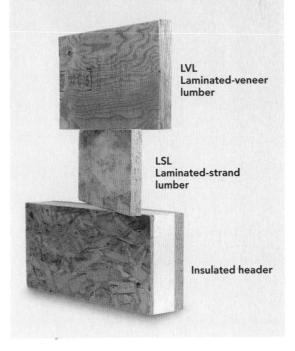

LVL
Laminated-veneer lumber

LSL
Laminated-strand lumber

Insulated header

The IRC lists spans for 9-in.-tall and 15-in.-tall box headers.

Two-sided box headers have greater spans than single-sided ones. All you have to do is follow a few conditions outlined in figure R602.7.3. Begin by framing in the cripple studs between the top plate and a flat 2x at the head of the rough opening, and support the flat 2x with the same number of jack studs the code requires for a conventional header of that length. Make sure the structural sheathing and top plate continue through the opening without any joints. Follow the fastening schedule: 8d common nails spaced every 3 in. and driven into the plates and the cripples. The sheathing must be a nominal ½ in. thick, and its strength axis must run parallel with the wall length. (The strength axis of most structural sheathing aligns with the sheets' long edges.) In many cases, the exterior wall sheathing alone can be used to create a one-sided box header.

For instance, in a 28-ft.-deep house with two stories and a center-bearing wall, a one-sided 9-in.-tall box header can span up to 3 ft.

Two-sided box headers give greater spans, but the interior structural panel is applied to the face of the studs, requiring you to pad out all the studs to match the plane before installing drywall. Alternatively, if you're framing walls from 2x6s, you can rip ½ in. off the plate, the tops of the king studs, and the head board. This isn't allowed with a 2x4 wall.

If you're already framing with ½-in. structural sheathing, then one-sided box headers are easy to incorporate. Just keep joints in the sheathing and top plate from falling above the opening, and nail the perimeter of the header properly. If the house is being sheathed with 7⁄16-in. OSB, you can install pieces of ½-in. panels just for box headers. The slight difference in thickness won't cause any problems.

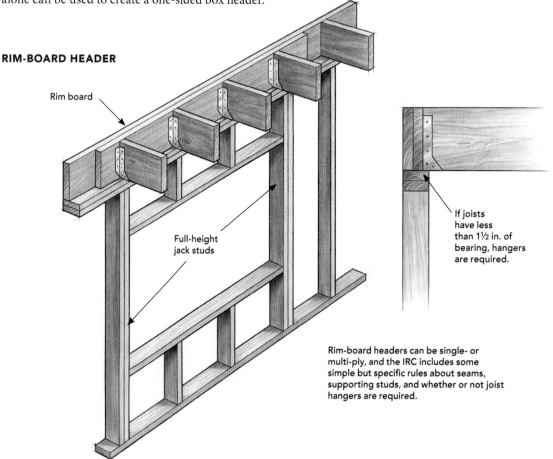

RIM-BOARD HEADER

Rim board

Full-height jack studs

If joists have less than 1½ in. of bearing, hangers are required.

Rim-board headers can be single- or multi-ply, and the IRC includes some simple but specific rules about seams, supporting studs, and whether or not joist hangers are required.

BUILDING UP HEADERS

When building multi-ply headers, you should start with the IRC's fastening schedule (table R602.3[1]), which covers two-ply headers with a ½-in. plywood or OSB spacer, presumably for a 2x4 wall. (No fastening schedule is given for other headers.) The schedule calls for 16d common nails at 16 in. o.c. or 16d box nails at 12 in. o.c. I run two rows of nails on 2x6 to 2x10 headers and add a third row in the middle of 2x12 headers.

In 2x6 walls, I usually frame double headers by sandwiching 2-in. rigid foam between 1¾-in. LVL stock or 2½-in. rigid foam between 2x stock. Because nails aren't long enough to penetrate both plies and the foam, I use 5-in. or 5½-in. FastenMaster FlatLOK or HeadLOK screws, or 5-in. Simpson Strong-Tie SDWS screws. The low-profile heads on these screws sit flush with the surfaces of the lumber, so they don't interfere with sheathing or drywall. I space the screws roughly 16 in. apart about 2 in. down from the edges of the header.

I rarely frame walls with 2x4s, but when I do, I use ½-in. rigid foam between the plies of built-up headers rather than OSB or plywood. Even though the R-value of the foam is small, it breaks the thermal bridge somewhat.

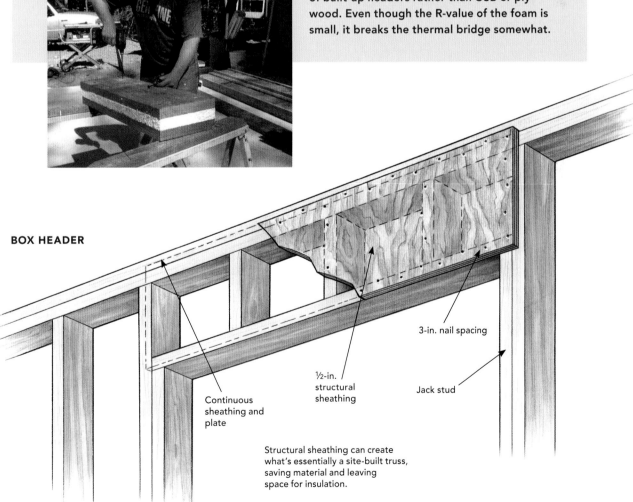

BOX HEADER

Continuous sheathing and plate

½-in. structural sheathing

3-in. nail spacing

Jack stud

Structural sheathing can create what's essentially a site-built truss, saving material and leaving space for insulation.

Laying Out Stud Walls

BY ANDY ENGEL

How you lay out the stud locations in a wall affects everything that comes after, from sheathing, to hanging drywall, to plumbing and HVAC rough-in, to trimming the interior. The stud layout is marked on the plates—the horizontal members at the top and bottom of a wall. It's worth taking the time to find straight, long stock for the plates, and to cut them accurately to length. The

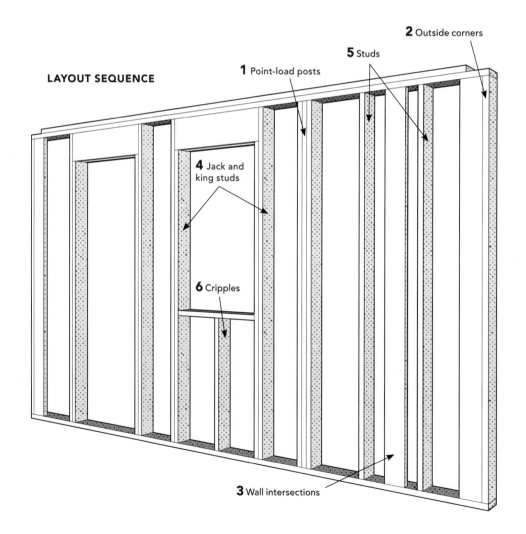

LAYOUT SEQUENCE

1 Point-load posts

2 Outside corners

5 Studs

4 Jack and king studs

6 Cripples

3 Wall intersections

1 MARK THE POINT LOADS FIRST. With the plates laid next to each other, mark the edge of all the studs in point-load posts using dimensions from the blueprints.

X MARKS THE SPOT. Every standard-height stud is marked on the plates with an X. With the two plates next to each other, you can quickly mark an X on each by making two Cs, one backward.

blueprints will rarely, if ever, specify the location of every stud, so the carpenter is expected to understand framing principles well enough to get the layout right regardless of the level of detail on the plans.

There are four things to consider when laying out a wall. The first is load path. Loads are the weight of rafters, floor joists, and beams that bear on the wall from above. Each of these needs at least one stud below it and often more than one in the case of beams and headers, which transfer loads around openings. The locations of these point loads—below beams, for example—as well as the number of studs required below each, should be called out on the plans. These

studs are usually nailed together into a post before installation. The studs of any wall above the first floor of a house should stack on the joists and studs below to form a load path all the way to the foundation. This isn't just a load-path consideration; stacked framing makes the job of the mechanical trades—running ducts, pipes, and wire—much easier.

The next consideration is the location of intersecting walls. When laying these out, be careful that you're measuring their position from the location indicated on the plans—it's very easy to mark the wrong side of an intersecting wall on a plate and inadvertently change a room dimension. Pay

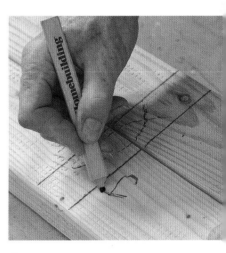

2 OUTSIDE CORNERS GET TWO STUDS. Nailed together in an L-shape, one stud is the outside nailer for sheathing, while the inner one will extend one stud thickness past the intersecting wall to serve as a drywall nailer.

3 BE CAREFUL AT INTERSECTIONS. Mark both edges of midplate wall intersections. For intersecting 2x4 walls, mark the plates to receive a 2x6 on the flat. The wider stud will extend past each side of the intersecting 2x4 to provide drywall nailing.

4 KINGS AND JACKS MARK WINDOWS AND DOORS. There's one full-height king stud on each side of an opening. Jack studs (marked with a J) are the header depth shorter than kings and form the inside of the opening. Wider openings usually have two or more jacks on each side.

5 REGULAR STUDS FOLLOW A REGULAR LAYOUT. The highlighted numbers on the tape—usually in red—indicate the common 16-in.-o.c. spacing, but layout requires the edges be marked, not the centers. To mark the edge of a 1½-in. stud, subtract ¾ in., and mark an X to the right.

particular attention to places such as alcoves for tubs, whose dimensions have no flexibility.

Next are window and door openings and the king and jack (or trimmer) studs that outline their rough openings. These should also be called out on the plans. Finally we have the common studs, which are spaced primarily to accommodate the wall sheathing edges, but also those of the drywall. This is where the layout marks on the tape measure come into play. Whether the framing is on 24-in. centers, 16-in. centers (usually highlighted in red on the tape), or 19.2-in. centers (highlighted with small black diamonds), these numbers represent the stud centers, whereas you'll be marking a stud edge, which is ¾ in. to one side or the other of the stud center. For a 16-in.-o.c. stud layout, for example, it doesn't matter whether you make a mark at 15¼ in. or 16¾ in., as long as you indicate to which side of your mark the stud should be located so that the center of the stud ends up 16 in. from the stud to either side.

6 FILL IN WITH CRIPPLES. Short studs called cripples support windows' rough sills. When a header doesn't completely fill the space below the top plate, cripples are used there, as well. Cripples fall on the stud layout, but are marked with a C.

Double-Stud Walls

BY RACHEL WAGNER

Energy-conscious builders pioneered double-stud walls after the oil-price shocks of the 1970s. This relatively low-tech method of building energy-efficient walls uses common materials and familiar assemblies. These walls have several benefits in addition to their high R-value: Thick cellulose-insulated walls are quiet, and many homeowners appreciate the deep window stools. In addition, the framing method virtually eliminates thermal bridging within the wall assembly, although there still can be thermal bridges at sills, top plates, and window and door openings.

The basic strategy is simple: An exterior wall is built from two parallel stud walls. Both stud walls and the space between them are filled with continuous insulation. The exterior is sheathed and finished conventionally, although a rain-screen siding detail is recommended (sidebar, p. 147). Of course, there are some important design and construction considerations, starting with the appropriate thickness.

One size does not fit all

You can vary the thickness of double-stud walls for each project or climate to achieve an overall R-value that fits. The R-value of dense-packed cellulose (the most common insulation used in double-stud walls) is about 3.7 or 3.8 per inch, so a 12-in. double-stud wall has an R-value of about 45.

Both the design of the building and your performance goals affect the optimum thickness of your walls. The walls might be 16 in. thick for a Passive House in Vermont, but only 10 in. thick for a low-energy house in Iowa. A bigger or more complicated building usually warrants thicker walls (with a higher R-value) than a small, simple building.

Wall construction can vary depending on the type of foundation, the type of floor system, and the preference of the builder or designer. For a slab on grade, a 2x6 outer wall allows the outer stud wall to be situated so that the framing bears on the slab and also extends past the slab edge to cover the vertical rigid insulation at the slab. With a basement, the double-stud wall sits on the floor framing, so both walls usually can be framed with 2x4s. Studs can be either 16 in. or 24 in. o.c.; be sure that the interior finish materials and the siding are compatible with the stud spacing.

One sill plate or two?

Separate stud walls with individual sill plates will be easier to construct and more energy efficient, but a shared bottom plate can be useful when framing on an insulated slab foundation. A shared top plate isn't required, but installing a continuous ¾-in. plywood top plate can meet fire-blocking requirements and make it easier to install floor or roof trusses.

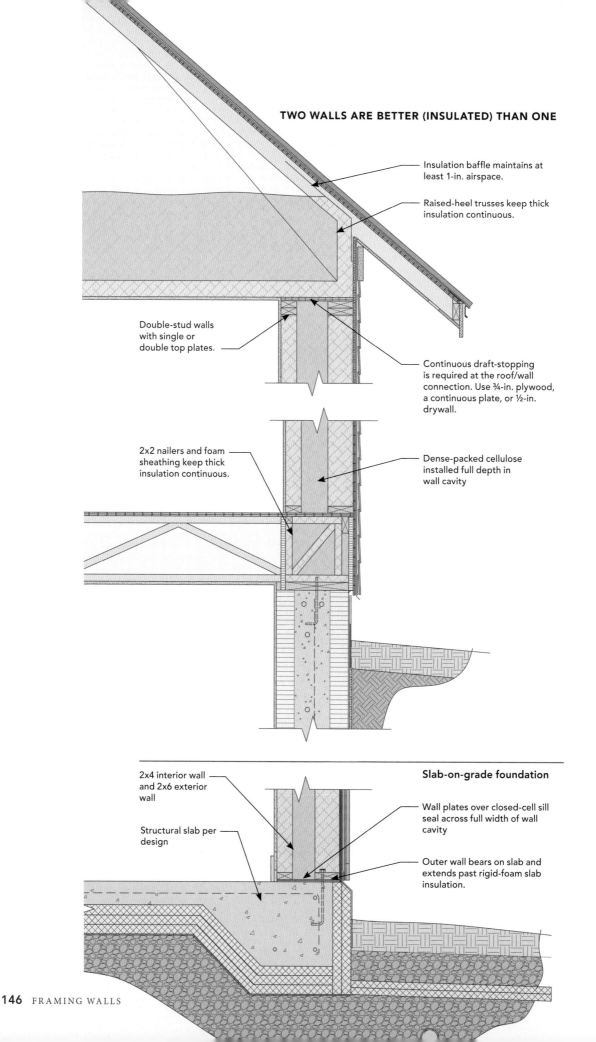

TWO WALLS ARE BETTER (INSULATED) THAN ONE

Insulation baffle maintains at least 1-in. airspace.

Raised-heel trusses keep thick insulation continuous.

Double-stud walls with single or double top plates.

Continuous draft-stopping is required at the roof/wall connection. Use ¾-in. plywood, a continuous plate, or ½-in. drywall.

2x2 nailers and foam sheathing keep thick insulation continuous.

Dense-packed cellulose installed full depth in wall cavity

Slab-on-grade foundation

2x4 interior wall and 2x6 exterior wall

Structural slab per design

Wall plates over closed-cell sill seal across full width of wall cavity

Outer wall bears on slab and extends past rigid-foam slab insulation.

Most framers erect the outer wall separately and first; this approach most resembles conventional stud-wall construction. When framing the inner wall, it is important to align window and door openings perfectly; the openings will be joined later using plywood box frames, like big gussets. The studs in the two walls can be either parallel or staggered, but they must line up at the openings. Parallel studs are nice for insulation netting and draft-stopping; of course, the studs won't be parallel at the corners. Some builders like to construct double-stud wall trusses using plywood gussets; in this case, the walls go up together.

Air-sealing still matters

Lots of insulation does not guarantee better energy performance. It's also essential to minimize air leaks within wall construction. This enhances energy performance and reduces the risk of moisture intrusion into the wall.

Be sure to define the interior air barrier, which can be drywall if you're using the airtight-drywall approach, a product such as MemBrain (www.certainteed.com), a layer of OSB under the drywall, or even polyethylene if you're building in a very cold climate. Continuously seal all joints and connections at seams, corners, floors, ceilings, and window and door openings. Seal around all electrical boxes, wire and conduit, and duct penetrations.

PERFORMANCE REQUIREMENTS FOR DOUBLE-STUD WALLS

FIRE BLOCKING
The International Residential Code (IRC section R302.11) requires draft-stopping in double-stud assemblies every 10 ft. (minimum) along the length of the wall, from bottom plate to top plate and covering the full depth of the double cavity, using ½-in. gypsum drywall or ¾-in. plywood. (Drywall is easier to cut and fit into place.) The code also requires fire blocking to keep the top of the wall assembly separate from the floor framing or attic spaces above. If you're not using a full-depth top plate that spans across both stud walls, install ½-in. drywall or ¾-in. plywood between the top plates, and fire-caulk the joints.

INSULATION
Current practices favor dense-packed cellulose or fiberglass blown through fabric into the wall. With thick cavities not fully divided into neat individual bays, it's important to maintain the required density of the insulation to prevent it from settling, which would leave an uninsulated gap at the top of the assembly. Some builders "net" each bay, fastening filter fabric across the depth of the two studs essentially to create individual full bays. Then they fasten the fabric across the front of the wall assembly, as is typical for dense-packing, and blow the insulation into each bay as they would for a single-stud wall. (If you want to use this technique, you must align the studs in both walls.) Another technique uses the horizontal draft-stopping as the containment for the insulation, although it is placed at intervals of 8 ft. o.c. instead of 10 ft. Filter fabric is then used only at the face of the framing.

MOISTURE
A double-stud wall slows heat loss from the building better than a single-stud wall, so the exterior sheathing will be colder and potentially wetter in winter than it would be in a typical single-stud wall. In most climates where a double-stud wall will be used, the code requires a vapor retarder on the warm side of the wall; vapor-retarder paint can satisfy this requirement. Plywood or structural fiberboard sheathing will give the wall a better chance to dry outward than OSB, and installing the siding over furring strips also helps the sheathing to stay dry.

Air-Sealed Mudsill Assembly

BY STEVE BACZEK

The mudsill is one of the most critical components of a successful Passive House. It involves a connection between dissimilar materials, and making such a connection airtight is a challenge. Even the best stemwall will have some imperfections. Also, the mudsill typically will be wet from its preservative treatment and from the lumberyard, and it will shrink as it dries. This means that there likely will be gaps between the wood and the concrete. Traditionally, this part of the building is sealed with a foam gasket. In a Passive House, however, even a minor gap is a major problem, so our assembly is a bit more complex.

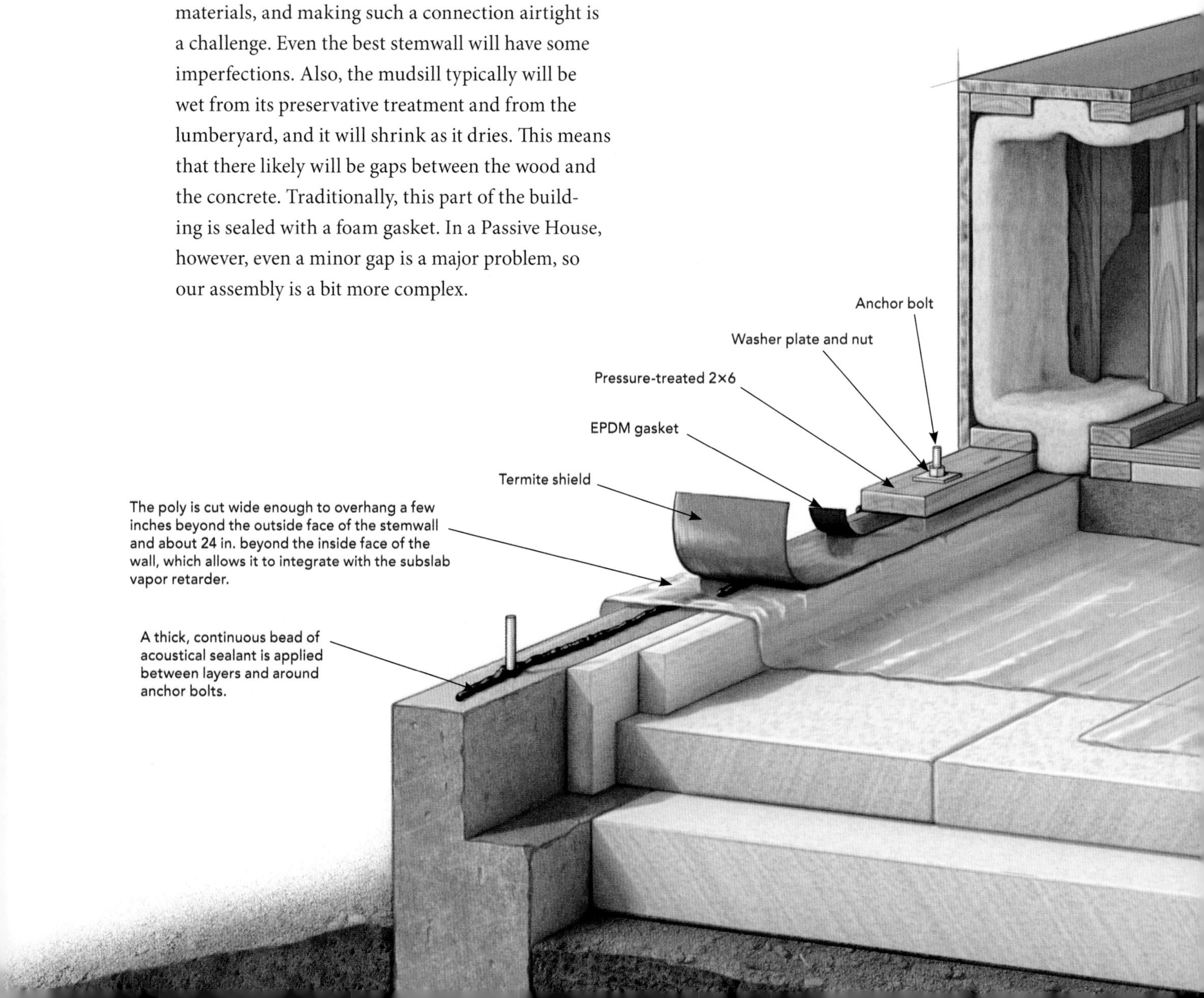

Anchor bolt

Washer plate and nut

Pressure-treated 2×6

EPDM gasket

Termite shield

The poly is cut wide enough to overhang a few inches beyond the outside face of the stemwall and about 24 in. beyond the inside face of the wall, which allows it to integrate with the subslab vapor retarder.

A thick, continuous bead of acoustical sealant is applied between layers and around anchor bolts.

PREP THE PLATE. To locate the bolts accurately, the mudsill is laid on edge across the top of the stemwall, and each bolt location is scribed onto the face of the 2x6.

NARROW WALLS REQUIRE OFFSET STRINGS. The tops of these stemwalls are only wide enough to carry the 2x6 walls, so the carpenters attach 2x spacer blocks to the stemwalls, and then they fasten an offset stringline to the blocks to use as a reference for measuring.

DRILL THE LAYERS AS A SANDWICH. Although they started out marking and boring through each layer separately, the carpenters quickly learned that it's faster to stack up the poly, termite shield, and 2x6 mudsill; clamp them together; and drill through everything at once.

THE GASKET IS TREATED SEPARATELY. The soft and stretchy EPDM gasket (sidebar, p. 152) tends to get snagged and wrapped up by a spinning drill bit, so after the other layers are drilled, the gasket is stapled to the underside of the mudsill and sliced with a utility knife at each bolt-hole location.

WHAT IT TAKES TO BE A PASSIVE HOUSE

THE PASSIVE HOUSE STANDARD aims to maximize passive energy gains while minimizing energy losses. This is achieved with superinsulation, high-performance windows and doors, minimal thermal bridging, strict airtightness of the building envelope, mechanical ventilation, and optimal passive-solar gain. To attain Passive House certification, all of the building compo- nents are individually scrutinized in the Passive House Planning Package (PHPP), an elaborate spreadsheet program, before any construction begins. The PHPP predicts the performance of the house before it's built. Once built, the house is tested by a third party to ensure that it has achieved three performance requirements.

AIR INFILTRATION

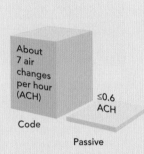

About 7 air changes per hour (ACH)

≤0.6 ACH

Code

Passive

Comparison: The IRC's current energy codes require houses to have no more than 7 air changes per hour (ACH) at 50 Pa.

BTU CONSUMPTION

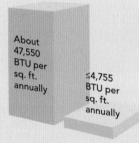

About 47,550 BTU per sq. ft. annually

≤4,755 BTU per sq. ft. annually

Comparison: That's roughly 90% less heating and cooling than is required in a similarly sized code-built house.

ENERGY USAGE

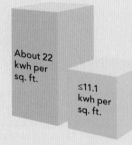

About 22 kwh per sq. ft.

≤11.1 kwh per sq. ft.

Comparison: This number which includes heating, cooling, and electricity, is roughly half that of a typical house.

STARTS GOOEY AND STAYS THAT WAY. The primary air-seal in this assembly is Tremco acoustical sealant. Highly elastic and sticky right out of the tube, this sealant won't harden over time like construction adhesives, so it creates a reliable air-seal at vulnerable joints.

PLASTIC COMES FIRST. After applying a thick, continuous bead of acoustical sealant to the top of the concrete, the carpenters lay the poly vapor retarder in place. They use hand pressure to push it firmly into the bead of sealant.

TERMITE SHIELD. Another bead of acoustical sealant is laid across the top of the poly before the termite shield, a copper-polymer composite membrane called YorkShield 106 TS (yorkmfg. com), is placed over it.

SEAL THE JOINTS. Before placing the next 2x6 sill, a thick bead of sealant is applied to the edge of any adjoining sill. This is a commonly overlooked weak spot in an air-sealed assembly.

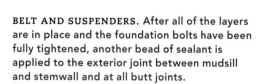

BELT AND SUSPENDERS. After all of the layers are in place and the foundation bolts have been fully tightened, another bead of sealant is applied to the exterior joint between mudsill and stemwall and at all butt joints.

GASKETS

Polyethylene gasket

EPDM gasket

TRADITIONALLY, THE MUDSILL IS LAID ATOP a ¼-in.-thick polyethylene gasket. Although this sill sealer does help to reduce air leakage between the sill and the concrete, it's far from airtight. On this house, the builders installed a soft rubber EPDM gasket (BG63) made by Conservation Technology (www.conservationtechnology.com). Unlike with poly gaskets, the manufacturer claims that its EPDM gaskets will stay flexible at extremely low temperatures and will respond well to shrinkage and swelling even after decades of compression.

This part of the build typically is done on the carpenters' first day, so it's often their first hands-on involvement with the extreme airtightness requirement of this kind of house. In most cases, the carpenters never will have built even close to a Passive House level of airtightness, so establishing a good mental standard for the job starts here.

The mudsill is a one-shot deal. This project relies on several blower-door tests to evaluate air leakage, but the first test won't happen until the walls and roof are in place and sheathed. By then, any air leakage at the mudsill is far more difficult to address. It needs to be right the first time; there is no second chance here.

Learning to love acoustical sealant

There are various sealants, gaskets, self-adhering membranes, and building tapes for air-sealing mudsills. Although we used a gasket in one layer of the mudsill assembly on this house—a belt-and-suspenders approach—most of the airtightness hinges on the use of Tremco acoustical sealant. Sold in tubes at specialty retailers and online, the black sealant installs easily with a caulk gun. It's exceed-

ingly sticky and highly elastic, and unlike construction adhesive, it never cures. While the gooey, get-everywhere sealant makes for an interesting job site (you'll want to keep a large bottle of Goof Off or Goo Gone on hand), it is the most effective air-sealing solution I have found.

One of the issues I have in sealing mudsills with a rubber gasket alone is the treatment of butt joints and changes in direction. A healthy bead of sealant eliminates any concern about gaps in these areas.

Every change has implications

In a Passive House, nailing down all of the building details before any principal construction work begins is exceedingly important. But even the best-laid plans are going to need last-minute tweaks. Here, the client feared that termites might move into the walls, where the double-stud framing would make it especially difficult to notice the infestation. In an effort to ease the client's mind while keeping with the builder's schedule, we decided to add a copper termite shield to the mudsill assembly. This termite shield later was trimmed back on the inside and covered with foam, eliminating the chance of a thermal bridge.

Shear Walls

BY ROB YAGID

Not every house needs to have shear walls integrated into the framing, but many do. In earthquake country, for example, shear walls help to strengthen houses so that they're far less likely to move under the severe lateral forces of a seismic event. Shear walls not only help to prevent catastrophic collapse, but they also help to prevent smaller-scale damage like cracked drywall and fractured tile. Shear walls play the same role in houses in high-wind zones. No matter the source of the force exerted on a house—atmospheric or tectonic—shear walls are simply designed to protect the home and its occupants.

A key component of seismic-retrofit work is the integration of site-built shear walls into the framing. To be able to construct a shear wall so that it performs properly and offers maximum strength, you need to know how it works.

Performance under pressure

Shear walls are designed to resist several forces simultaneously, and those forces can shift in opposing directions at any given moment. Shown on p. 154 is an example of what can happen when a conventional wall experiences the stress of an earthquake or hurricane.

Lateral. The primary lateral force from an earthquake or high-wind event causes simultaneous uplift, compression, and sliding forces.

Uplift. Lateral forces try to roll the wall off the foundation, creating uplift on one end of the wall assembly.

Compression. As one end of the wall is experiencing uplift, the opposite end is under compression. These loads alternate as the building shakes back and forth.

Sliding resistance. The few anchor bolts that are present try to counteract the lateral force, which tries to slide the wall off the foundation, but the bolts are ineffective.

One way to build a shear wall

Extra foundation hardware, 4x4 posts, structural plywood, and a lot of nails help walls to resist the forces of earthquakes and high winds. These components shouldn't be added to a wall without the advice of an engineer, however. An engineer will optimize a shear wall's design to meet the specific demands of a house, which will dictate details like nail size and nailing schedule, hardware placement, and blocking size and orientation.

WHY WE NEED SHEAR WALLS

EARTHQUAKE/HURRICANE FORCES ON A WALL

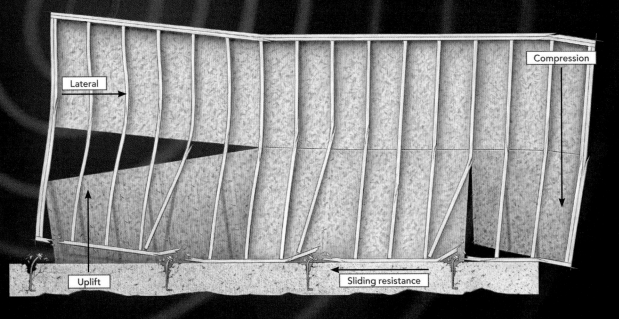

Compression

Lateral

Uplift

Sliding resistance

SHEAR WALL

Placing 4x4 posts behind vertical sheathing joints is the best way to retain shear-wall integrity.

To increase the stiffness of the wall assembly and to hold the shear wall together, ½-in. plywood should extend from the top of the top plate to the bottom of the bottom plate.

Edge nails placed every 3 in. should not be driven within ⅜ in. of the edge of the plywood.

Hold-down hardware at the ends of each shear wall reinforces the connection between the wall and foundation, and keeps the wall from overturning due to uplift forces.

Full round-head nails attach plywood to studs. Studies show that nails set flush to plywood surfaces perform far better than countersunk nails. Never use screws, which are more brittle than nails.

Anchor bolts set with 3-in. by 3-in. washer plates keep first-floor walls from sliding off the foundation.

The sill plates and foundation walls must be in solid condition to support the shear wall when under compression.

A Slick Approach to Straightening Walls

BY ROE A. OSBORN

The framer's version of the classic chicken-or-egg question relates to straightening walls. Is straightening the final step in first-floor wall construction or the start of the second-floor deck? I think it's the latter, and here's why. Let's say you finish framing the walls on a Thursday. Friday it rains, so you don't work. You're off for the weekend, and Monday is a holiday. If you'd straightened the walls on Thursday, they would have had four days to move around in the wind and weather, and you'd probably have to tweak them again before framing the floor above. The floor framing locks in your straightening efforts, so that's why I associate straightening walls with framing the second floor.

The project shown here is a good illustration of how to straighten walls. Built to engineers' specs that satisfy the 110-mph wind-zone requirement, this framing is much beefier than normal, and therefore a little tougher to push back into a straight line. Still, with this technique, much of the work is a one-person job.

Create a reference line with string

Over the years, I've seen lots of methods, special tools, and jigs for straightening walls, but in my opinion, the springboard method I learned when I first started building houses still works best. It's a two-step process that starts with stringing the walls.

Begin by nailing 2x blocks to the inside corners of all four walls. Then drive two additional nails partway into each block (photo, p. 156). These nails act as anchor pegs for the string. Many framers use strong mason's twine for stringing because it can be stretched extremely taut. A chalkline can work just as well, though, and it has the advantage of having a hook on the end that can slip over the bottom nail on one block.

Tie or hook the string to the bottom nail, and lead it over the top nail. Then stretch the string as tight as possible to the block at the other end of the wall. At this end, lead the string over the top nail, pull it tight, and wrap it several times around the bottom nail. Then wrap the string back over itself on the nail to keep it tight. The trick here is not to tie a knot that might have to be untied later. You now have a straight reference line running the length of the wall.

Let kicker boards do the work

Remove the temporary bracing used to hold the wall upright. (Unless conditions are very windy, even a fairly long wall should stand on its own for now.) The trick is to push the wall in or out to make it perfectly parallel to the string, which is where the springboards come in. For springboard material, I use 12-ft. 1x8 rough-sawn pine boards because they're flexible, strong, and inexpensive. Also, they

Top plate

Gauge block

Springboard

Stringline

Kicker

2x blocks

A ONE-MAN JOB. To straighten the wall, 12-ft.-long springboards are tacked underneath the top plate, then bowed down and tacked to the deck. Shorter kicker boards nailed beneath the springboards are used to manipulate the curve of the springboards, which in turn move the wall in or out. A taut string held off the top plate by blocks creates a guide that can be checked with 2x scrap.

come in handy around the job site after they've fulfilled their springing duties. Taller walls require longer boards.

Walls are usually straightened one at a time, and it really doesn't matter which one is first. Choose a wall, and position springboards every 8 ft. or so along the wall. Long headers at rough openings for windows and doors may require a springboard at each end. Also, be conscious of any hinge points, such as sheathing joints, that would make the wall bend. This is particularly important with tall walls.

Starting at one end of the wall, nail one end of a springboard to the underside of the top plate. Secure the other end to the deck, giving the board a slight downward bend as you nail it. This actually pushes on the wall, which means you'll likely be letting in the wall later.

Now nail the bottom of a 4-ft.-long 1x8 kicker to the deck below the springboard. Bring the top of the kicker snug against the springboard, but don't nail that end yet. Pushing the kicker board in or out changes the amount of arc in the springboard, which in turn moves the wall in or out.

Once the springboards are in place, you can begin to straighten the wall. Slide a 2x gauge block up to the string, then push on the kicker until the gauge block just slips under the string. Then drive nails through the springboard and into the end of the kicker to hold the wall straight.

After working down the length of one wall, sight the string and plate for a final check. This is your last opportunity to make sure the walls are dead straight before locking them in with the second-floor framing. The slightest deviation in the wall can turn into a major wave once the exterior siding and trim are applied.

1 START AT THE TOP PLATE. Placed at approximately 8-ft. intervals, springboards are first nailed to the underside of the top plate.

The top plate pushes out.

Push down on the springboard.

2 LOAD THE SPRINGBOARD. With the board's lower end on the deck, push down on the middle of the board and tack that end in place.

3 INSTALL THE KICKER. The board that moves the springboard is known as a kicker. Typically a 4-ft. length of 1x8, it's positioned near the center of the springboard. Tack one end to the deck, and bring the other end up snug against the springboard.

The top plate pulls back in.

Push down on the kicker.

4 GAUGE THE MOVEMENT OF THE TOP PLATE. While sliding the kicker against the springboard with one hand, check the gap between the string and the top plate with a 2x4. Sliding the kicker away from the wall should pull the wall toward the line.

5 NAIL IT HOME. When the gauge indicates that the wall section is straight, drive a nail down through the springboard into the kicker to lock its position.

SOMETIMES YOU NEED MORE LEVERAGE

IN MOST CASES, SPRINGBOARDS CAN EASILY STRAIGHTEN A WALL. But sometimes more force is required, especially near the end of a wall. A site-built lever lets you apply that force in a controlled fashion. Nail a diagonal 2x brace to a stud near the top of the wall at the trouble spot, and nail a long 2x block to the deck next to the loose end of the brace. Now nail a 2x lever to the block and to the brace. Pull back on the lever as someone else gauges the string. When the wall is straight, nail the bottom of the brace to the block to hold the wall in position.

6 DOUBLE-CHECK THE STRING. Once all springboards have been adjusted, go back and sight down the stringline to make sure that the wall is straight. Now is the time for any last-minute tweaks, before the top plates are locked into position by the joists above.

Bringing Back Balloon-Frame Construction

BY PAUL BIEBEL

I grew up in a large, vintage New England house with a high-ceiling attic that was every kid's dream clubhouse. There was a 2-ft.-high kneewall around the perimeter of the attic, and studs protruded through the flooring. I didn't know then that this type of framing, balloon-frame construction, meant that the wall studs ran uninterrupted from the top of the foundation to the bottom of the roof rafters. But I learned that if I got close to the 4-in.-wide chasm around the perimeter of the attic, I could feel a breeze blowing up from below (my first experience with the stack effect) and that if I dropped a marble in that chasm, I could hear it rattling all the way down through the wall and later find it waiting on the basement floor.

Balloon framing was a dying practice back then and is essentially extinct today. That's because in the 1920s, builders began framing houses using a method called platform framing, by which the first floor is built and then used as a platform to erect the walls, which support the next floor, and so on. The reasons for the switch were many: easier framing without scaffolding, better resistance against fire jumping floors, and a general decline in the availability of tall, straight, quality framing lumber.

Nowadays, the challenge we face in building custom homes is in finding the most cost-effective way to build the highest-performing shell with the smallest renewable system necessary to provide 100% of the heat, cooling, and domestic hot water for our

TRADITIONAL VS. DOUBLE-STUD BALLOON FRAME

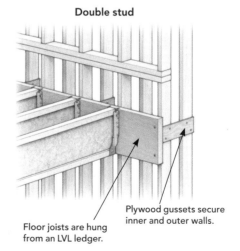

Traditional

Ribband provides support.

Floor joists are nailed to wall studs.

Double stud

Floor joists are hung from an LVL ledger.

Plywood gussets secure inner and outer walls.

1 ATTACHING THE FLOOR SYSTEM to the wall studs (either eave or gable) with a ledger eliminates the difficult-to-insulate rim-joist area that's common to platform-framed walls.

2 CONTINUOUS EAVE-WALL STUDS eliminate the structural hinge point of short upper-story stud walls, offering better resistance against the outward force of the roof rafters above.

3 UNINTERRUPTED DOUBLE-STUD WALL CAVITIES provide ample room for faster and easier routing of all mechanicals, and they allow for lots of dense-pack insulation, creating a high-performance, low-cost wall.

clients. Ironically, I've discovered that balloon-framed walls fit this need nicely, as long as the design is updated with a few modern construction details and allows enough depth for adequate insulation. In short, I prefer to build balloon-framed double-stud walls, which represent an excellent balance of cost, familiarity, and performance.

Old meets new to create an ideal thermal assembly

Although double-stud walls are certainly not the norm in modern building, they are far from ground-breaking and have been used by progressive builders for decades. As with any building system, methods for their construction vary; in addition, your code official may require an engineer's stamp.

Our process starts with two independently framed 2x4 stud walls set with about a 4¼-in. space between. When we're able to frame all the walls on-site, we build and stand each one separately. If the framing happens in the dead of winter, as on this project, then we frame many of the walls off-site and truck them in for faster on-site assembly. In those cases, we frame the inner and outer faces of the walls at the same time, using 2x12 plates at the top and bottom. On gable walls, we do some of the infill framing after the walls have been raised and the roof trusses installed, making it easier to air-seal the connection between wall and roof.

The thing that pushes the envelope, though, is the integration of the balloon-frame concept. Rather than framing the double-stud walls in the platform fashion, we build the walls tall enough to run from the first-floor bottom plates to the second-floor top plates in a single push, with the floor system hung from a ledger. Now, other than the plywood gussets between studs (and 2x12 plates at the top and bottom, if included), thermal bridging between the exterior wall and interior wall is negligible. This approach also eliminates the weak hinge point of short-stud walls in the upstairs of a 1½-story house.

UNDERSTAND THE DESIGN DETAILS

DOUBLE-STUD WALLS ARE NEW TERRITORY for many builders, and balloon framing may be another layer of unfamiliarity on top of that. There are a few things to keep in mind when hashing out the details.

TIE THE WALLS TOGETHER
It's best for both walls to be connected so that they aren't working independently of each other. They can be tied together at two or three points between the floor and the ceiling using ½-in.-thick, 4-in. by 11¼-in. plywood gussets. It's important to get the inside and outside studs aligned with each other so that these gussets are easy to install.

FIRE BLOCKING IS BUILT IN
The building inspector has the final word, but GreenFiber's Cocoon cellulose insulation has an ICC Evaluation Service Report stating that the product is a code-compliant alternative to conventional means of fire blocking, so there shouldn't be a need for solid blocking. Netting between pairs of studs guides cellulose installation.

KNOW WHICH WALL IS LOAD BEARING
The author likes the interior half of the double-stud wall to carry the structural load from above, which means that it supports the floor joists and has the structural headers. If it's installed over an insulated slab, the portion of rigid foam directly under the plates should be high-compressive-strength foam, such as Amvic SilveRboard.

DOES IT PAY?

We ran the numbers to see how the balloon-framed double-stud wall compares to a wall assembly of 2x6s with closed-cell spray foam in the cavities and 2 in. of rigid foam on the exterior. Factoring in materials and labor, we found that the 2x6 wall cost about 14% more than the double-stud wall, despite offering a lower R-value.

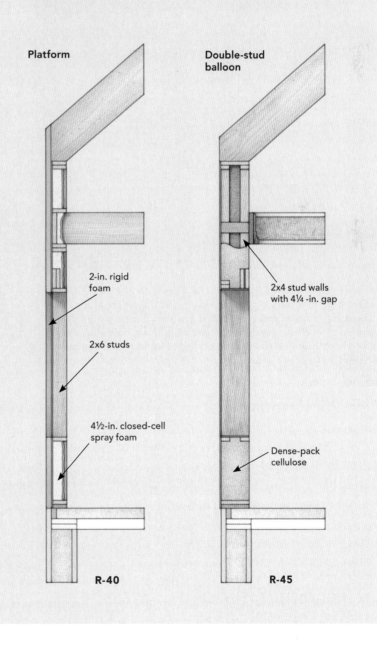

Platform

Double-stud balloon

2-in. rigid foam

2x4 stud walls with 4¼-in. gap

2x6 studs

4½-in. closed-cell spray foam

Dense-pack cellulose

R-40

R-45

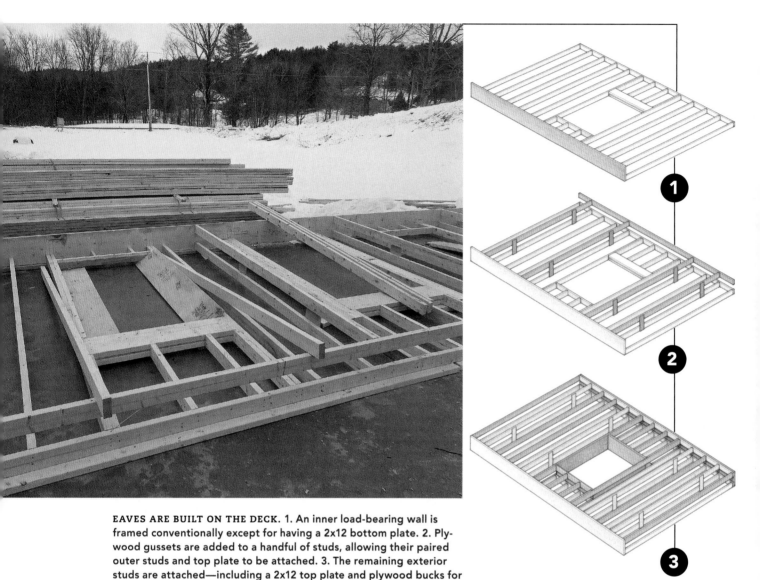

EAVES ARE BUILT ON THE DECK. 1. An inner load-bearing wall is framed conventionally except for having a 2x12 bottom plate. **2.** Plywood gussets are added to a handful of studs, allowing their paired outer studs and top plate to be attached. **3.** The remaining exterior studs are attached—including a 2x12 top plate and plywood bucks for windows and doors—before sheathing, taping, and standing the wall.

Caveats to consider

When working with double-stud walls of any kind, you must know which wall is bearing the weight of the house. I prefer to have the interior wall be load bearing, but an exterior bearing wall is possible if you change the way the floor system attaches. This approach could also affect foundation details when using insulated concrete forms (ICFs).

You may also find that engineers get nervous when asked to approve a plan in which the floor joists are hung from a structural ledger attached to the wall studs. I always thought that engineers relied solely on math (and when done properly, the math works fine here), but I'm learning that intuition plays a role as well. In some cases, I have been asked to beef up the carrying studs to 4x4s instead of 2x4s. When I asked why, the engineer simply replied, "Because it makes me feel better." Since the engineers are the ones who have to sign off in order for me to get a building permit, I just do what they tell me. For interior-design reasons, the floor joists on this project run the length of the building, but this unconventional floor-joist direction isn't related to the double-stud or balloon-frame methods.

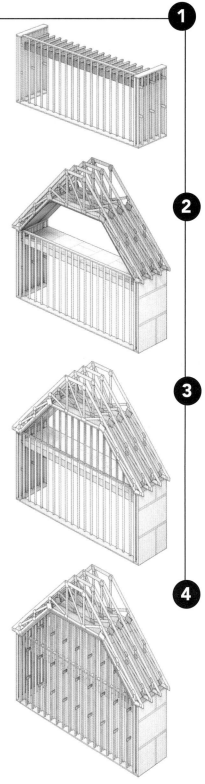

GABLES ARE FINISHED IN PLACE. 1. A gable wall begins with the same inner wall on a 2x12 plate, but then it is tipped into place to allow the floor-joist ledger to be attached. **2.** Next come the roof trusses, which are sheathed and taped on their underside for air-sealing purposes. **3.** The top half of the inner wall is then infilled. **4.** Full-height exterior wall studs are added, and the outside of the wall is sheathed and taped.

Wherever a double-frame wall encounters a window or door opening, I prefer to install ¾-in. by 11¼-in. plywood bucks around the inside of the rough opening. The plywood serves as a solid connection between both walls for installing the door or the window, thus providing a stable subplane for attaching the trim. Without it, the walls could move slightly over several years of drying, which would wreak havoc with jambs and casings. A word of caution: When framing door and window bucks using this system, you've got to tweak the size of each rough opening to allow for the additional thickness of the plywood.

Framing Roofs

Laying Out and Cutting Common Rafters

BY ANDY ENGEL

Although trusses dominate new construction in most parts of the country, traditional cut rafters are still the go-to approach to roof framing in some areas. They're also common in remodeling work and in small jobs such as entry-porch roofs.

Laying out rafters involves some math, but only for the first one. After it's been laid out and cut and its fit has been checked, it serves as a pattern for the rest. The two starting points for any rafter are the roof pitch—that is, the rise and run—and the building width. The run, or horizontal part, is always 12 (except in the case of a hip rafter), but the rise, or vertical part, varies. For example, an 8-in-12 (or 8-pitch) roof angle would rise 8 in. for every 12 in. of run. The second starting point is the building width. Even when you're working from a set of building plans, which list this dimension, always verify it by measuring between the top wall plates, from the outside face of the sheathing on one side to the outside face of the sheathing on the other.

When you have these two pieces of information, you can then determine the rafter length and lay out the cuts.

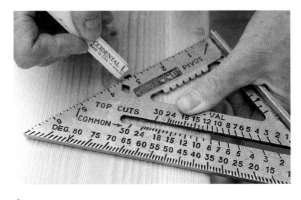

1 MARK THE RIDGE PLUMB CUT. Hold the pivot point of the rafter square on a straight piece of rafter stock. Using the "common" line, align the number corresponding to your pitch with the edge of the stock, and mark the ridge cut. Flip the square to the other side to complete the mark.

2 MAKE THE RIDGE PLUMB CUT. Use a sharp blade in a circular saw to split the layout line. Cutting up from the bottom of the rafter leaves a splinter-free edge that you'll appreciate when using this rafter as a template later on.

RAFTER ANATOMY

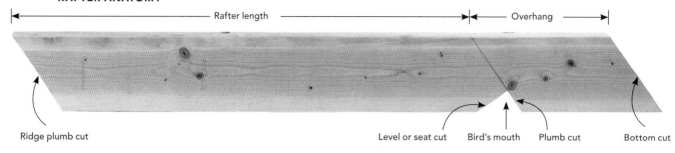

← Rafter length → | ← Overhang →

Ridge plumb cut | Level or seat cut | Bird's mouth | Plumb cut | Bottom cut

3 MARK THE LENGTH. Hook a tape measure on the point of the ridge cut, and pull the tape along the top of the rafter. Mark both the calculated rafter length and the overhang.

4 LAY OUT THE BIRD'S MOUTH AND BOTTOM PLUMB CUTS. Using the same technique as for marking the ridge cut, mark plumb lines for the bird's mouth and the bottom of the overhang.

Doing the math

Let's say that the measurement between the outside of the plates for an 8-in-12 entry-porch roof is 6 ft. Each rafter spans half that distance, so the theoretical total run (the horizontal distance the rafter spans) is 3 ft., or 36 in. From that, you have to deduct half the thickness of the ridge board to find the actual run. In most cases, a ridge board is a 2x that's one or two sizes deeper than the rafters (to provide enough depth for the full cut end of the rafter to bear on the ridge, a code requirement). The actual width of a 2x ridge is 1½ in., so deduct half of that, ¾ in., from the theoretical total run of 36 in. Actual run: 36 in. – ¾ in. = 35¼ in.

The rafter length is the diagonal measurement along the top edge of the rafter from its tip to a point directly above the outside of the wall plate. There are two simple ways to find it. The first is to plug the numbers into a construction calculator or app. For

the example of an 8-in-12 roof, enter 8 Pitch, then 35¼ in. Run. Press the Diag key to get the rafter length.

Alternatively, you can use the table on a framing square and some fourth-grade math. Most framing squares have a line labeled "Length of common rafter per foot [of] run." Follow that line to below the number that represents the roof pitch (here, 8), and find the rafter length per foot of run—in this case, 14.42 in. Because it's easier to do the math in inches

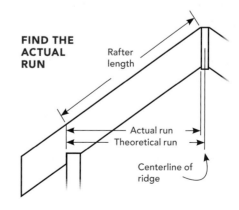

FIND THE ACTUAL RUN

Rafter length

Actual run
Theoretical run

Centerline of ridge

5 MARK THE LEVEL CUT. Align the inside of the square's flange with the plumb cut, and align the number corresponding to the combined width of the wall plate and the thickness of any sheathing with the bottom of the rafter. Mark the cut.

6 CUT THE BIRD'S MOUTH. Make both the level and the plumb cuts, splitting the lines and stopping at the corner. Many carpenters overcut the corner so that the scrap drops out, but this weakens the rafter.

7 FINISH THE BIRD'S MOUTH. Use a handsaw, reciprocating saw, or jigsaw to complete the plumb and level cuts.

8 MARK THE REST OF THE RAFTERS. The first rafter serves as a template for the others. Stop blocks screwed to the top of it speed placement. Cut two rafters, and then check their fit before cutting the entire roof.

rather than feet and inches, I convert the length per foot of run to length per inch of run.

Find the rafter length per inch of run by dividing the length per foot of run by 12:

$$14.42 \div 12 = 1.2 \text{ in.}$$

Find the rafter length by multiplying the length per inch of run by the actual run:

$$1.2 \times 35.25 = 42.3 \text{ in. } (42^5/_{16} \text{ in.})$$

You also need to find the rafter length for any overhang beyond the outside of the wall plate. The process for that is essentially the same as finding the rafter length, except that there's no ridge. Deduct the thickness of the fascia from the actual run. Once the rafter length is dialed in, it's time to lay out a rafter.

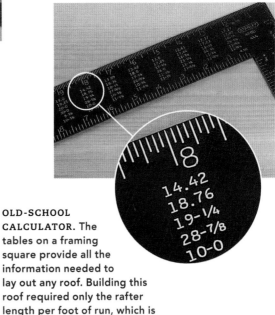

OLD-SCHOOL CALCULATOR. The tables on a framing square provide all the information needed to lay out any roof. Building this roof required only the rafter length per foot of run, which is found under the number that corresponds to the roof pitch.

Perfect Roof Rafters

BY SAM KOERBER

My process for framing a roof starts the same as anybody else's: laying out and cutting a pattern rafter, which I then use as a template to cut the rest of the rafters to make up the roof frame. Just like everybody else, I choose a flat, straight, and dry piece of stock for the pattern rafter, which I crown so that any natural arch is facing up when installed, and I set the piece atop a pair of sturdy sawhorses that are at a comfortable working height. From there, I get a bit more fussy than most with the layout, which I believe pays off big time in terms of the quality of my frames.

PATTERN RAFTER

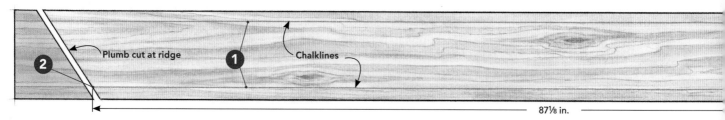

2

Plumb cut at ridge

1

Chalklines

87⅛ in.

Lessons learned from timber framing

Most of the time, framers use a 6-in. rafter square to lay out the plumb and seat cuts of a rafter. But two practices on recent jobs have convinced me to change up my approach. First, I've begun to incorporate components of timber framing into otherwise stick-framed houses; second, I do exposed rafter tails on most builds. Timber framing has taught me to use chalklines and a framing square for accurate layout on boards that don't have a reliable straight edge for reference. It also has taught me that a knife makes crisper layout lines than a pencil. Those same layout techniques have improved the consistency of the exposed rafter tails, ensuring that they not only look crisp and uniform but that they line up nicely without trimming and shimming once in place. Now, even on roofs without exposed rafter tails, I use this technique because it works better than the conventional methods.

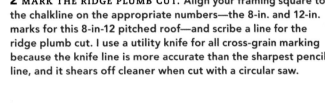

1 START OFF STRAIGHT. Mark 1 in. and 8 in. from the top edge on both ends of a 2x10, then snap a crisp chalkline between each pair of marks (0.5mm string is best) to create dead-straight reference lines.

2 MARK THE RIDGE PLUMB CUT. Align your framing square to the chalkline on the appropriate numbers—the 8-in. and 12-in. marks for this 8-in-12 pitched roof—and scribe a line for the ridge plumb cut. I use a utility knife for all cross-grain marking because the knife line is more accurate than the sharpest pencil line, and it shears off cleaner when cut with a circular saw.

3 FOLLOW THE LINE. Measure from the intersection of the chalkline and plumb cut—starting from the 1-in. mark for accuracy—to mark the rafter length. Adjust this line by half the thickness of the ridge to mark the plumb line that represents the sheathing's outside face.

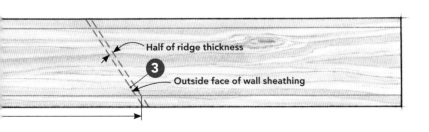

Half of ridge thickness

3

Outside face of wall sheathing

FINDING THE RAFTER LENGTH IS EASY

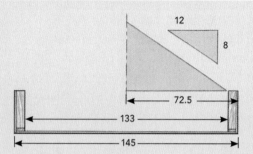

4 SQUARE UP FOR THE SEAT CUT. The bird's mouth is 6 in. wide—the combined width of the top plate and the wall sheathing—and referenced off the line that marks the rafter length.

ALL YOU NEED TO FIND THE LENGTH of a rafter is the width of the building, the desired roof pitch, and a basic calculator. The math may look intimidating at first, but go through the steps once and you'll see how easy it is.

Measure between the insides of the plates at the bottom of the wall (the easiest place to get an accurate read), and then add in the plate width and sheathing thickness:

133 in. (plate to plate) + 12 in. (total combined width of plates and sheathing) = 145 in.

A standard gable has two rafters that meet in the middle, so divide this number in half:

145 in. ÷ 2 = a rafter run of 72.5 in.

The roof pitch provides the next two numbers in the calculation. We want an 8-in-12 pitch, so multiply the run by 8, then divide the result by 12 to get the rise:

(72.5 × 8) ÷ 12 = a rafter rise of 48.33 in.

The key formula here is $a^2 + b^2 = c^2$. Plugging the run and rise into the formula lets you solve for c, the rafter length:

$72.5^2 + 48.33^2 = 7592.0389$

Hit the $\sqrt{\,}$ to find the square root, which is 87.134 in.

Carpenters don't deal in decimals, but converting the 0.134 remainder into 16ths is simple:

0.134 × 16 = 2, which is 2/16, or 1/8 in.

The final calculated rafter length is 87 1/8 in.

5 ADD THE OVERHANG. Reference your framing square off the plumb cut of the bird's mouth to calculate the desired amount of overhang, which is measured perpendicular from the bird's mouth plumb cut.

6 CUT THE TAILS. Use the chalkline as a reference when marking the depth of the notches on the top and bottom of the tail, and connect them with a sharp pencil, which won't wander to follow the grain.

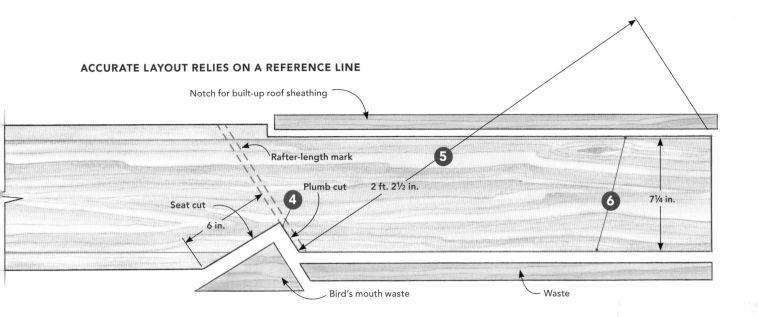

ACCURATE LAYOUT RELIES ON A REFERENCE LINE

Notch for built-up roof sheathing

Rafter-length mark

4

Seat cut

Plumb cut

6 in.

2 ft. 2½ in.

5

6

7¼ in.

Bird's mouth waste

Waste

MAKE CUTS WITH CARE, STARTING WITH THE BIRD'S MOUTH. Penciled-in arrows ensure that the seat and plumb cuts are made on the right side of the knife line. Stop the sawblade where the lines intersect to avoid overcutting.

NEXT COME THE CUTOUTS. Working from the plumb cut in, cut along the pencil lines to create the clean-cut 2x8 rafter tail.

FINISH UP WITH A CHISEL. A few whacks on the end of a sharp chisel make quick work of removing the waste from the corner of the bird's mouth.

Lumber, even the dimensioned stock we use for framing, is far from perfect. Referencing the ridge, seat, and other cuts off the edge of a board can throw off the layout more than you might think. Wany edges from the milling process, natural dips and humps in the board, and knots and other grain patterns all affect the trueness of a board edge. The conventional approach means trying to fit a long 2x between walls and roof when the layout of the angles is based only on the 6 in. of wood that is directly in

contact with the rafter square. Snapping your reference lines eliminates the inaccuracies.

Trust your rafter

Does such a fussy level of accuracy really matter with rough framing? My answer is that it's not about being perfect for the sake of perfection; it's about making the rest of the job go easier. If I'm confident that my rafters are laid out and cut to a high level of accuracy, I can trust them. This way, if they don't

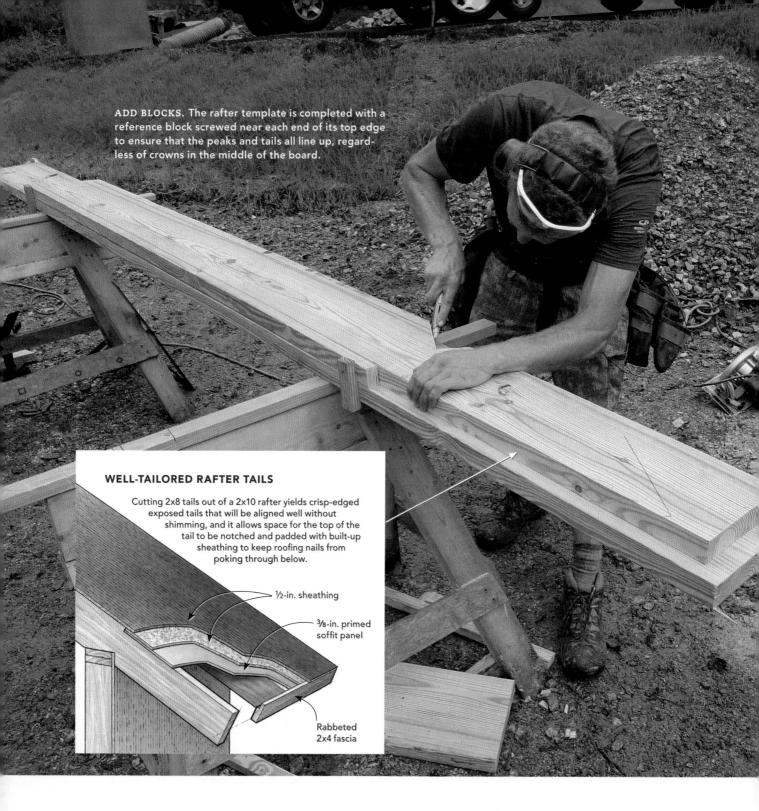

WELL-TAILORED RAFTER TAILS

Cutting 2x8 tails out of a 2x10 rafter yields crisp-edged exposed tails that will be aligned well without shimming, and it allows space for the top of the tail to be notched and padded with built-up sheathing to keep roofing nails from poking through below.

½-in. sheathing

⅜-in. primed soffit panel

Rabbeted 2x4 fascia

fit perfectly, I have a clue that something else in my framing is out of whack and needs to be adjusted. Maybe the top plate is a little crooked, the walls are slightly out of plumb, or the ridge board is cupped, crooked, or set too high or too low. Two wrongs don't make a right, and correcting these other components makes more sense to me than altering the ridge or seat cuts of a perfect rafter to fit a problematic frame.

I've found this process to be well worth the extra time spent doing layout. It's satisfying to be able to maintain control over the building throughout the roof-framing process.

Building Craftsman-Style Brackets

BY GARY M. KATZ

I've always been taken with the Craftsman style. I especially like the pillowed look of the style's multistep brackets: big, sturdy pieces of decorative joinery used to support deep eave overhangs and small roofs. When I designed my new shop and guest cabin, I wanted to include lots of them as eave supports. Most of the brackets I've seen have a diagonal brace that's mortised into the upper beam and lower post, and the mortises are cut at the same angle as the brace. I didn't want to do all that chiseling and sawing for 20 brackets. Instead, I designed my brackets so that all the dadoes could be cut with a router and a template and all the braces could be cut on a miter saw and notched on a tablesaw.

Make templates first

The siding I used on my house and shop is reclaimed beetle-kill pine that's milled and prefinished by Teton West, a lumber company in Wyoming, so I bought 4x6 beam stock for the brackets and exterior trim from them, too. The only thing I had to do is rip the stock down to the right size. I used a 1-in.-wide carbide blade on my bandsaw to make perfectly straight cuts.

ADD A CUSTOM TOUCH WHERE YOUR ROOF NEEDS A LITTLE SUPPORT. The brackets shown here support a small gable roof that shelters an exterior door on the author's shop.

175

BRACKET ANATOMY

Each bracket was dry-fit, then stained and assembled in place.

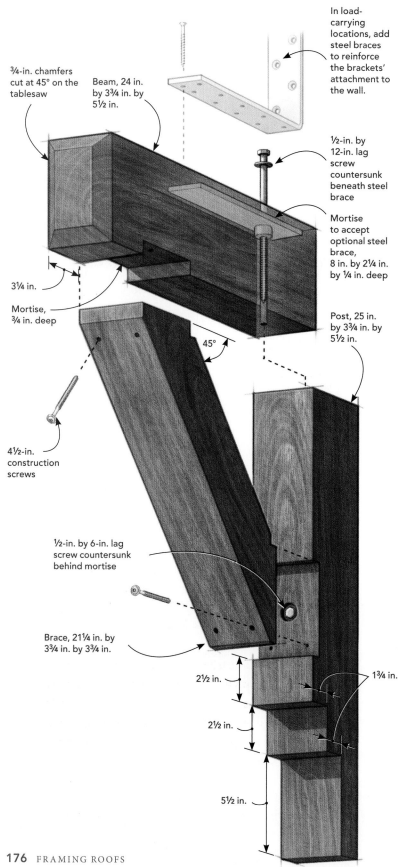

¾-in. chamfers cut at 45° on the tablesaw

Beam, 24 in. by 3¾ in. by 5½ in.

In load-carrying locations, add steel braces to reinforce the brackets' attachment to the wall.

½-in. by 12-in. lag screw countersunk beneath steel brace

Mortise to accept optional steel brace, 8 in. by 2¼ in. by ¼ in. deep

3¼ in.

Mortise, ¾ in. deep

45°

Post, 25 in. by 3¾ in. by 5½ in.

4½-in. construction screws

½-in. by 6-in. lag screw countersunk behind mortise

Brace, 21¼ in. by 3¾ in. by 3¾ in.

2½ in.

1¾ in.

2½ in.

5½ in.

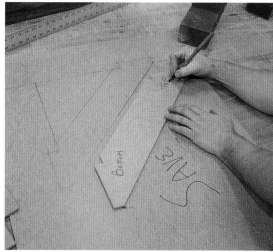

RETAIN CONSISTENCY USING TEMPLATES AND JIGS. The parts for the brackets were made in the shop with an efficient system of templates and jigs. Begin by drawing each of the three parts of the bracket full scale on ¼-in. hardboard, and cut it out as a template.

ONE-PASS NOTCH. After mitering both ends of the diagonal brace, notch the ends with a dado blade mounted in a tablesaw.

ROUTER JIG MAKES QUICK MORTISES. Used with a plunge router, this jig guides the cuts for the brace mortises. The workpiece is captured between adjustable stops, which can be repositioned for the longer vertical post.

FAST CUTS ON THICK STOCK. To cut the pillowed steps in the bracket post, first crosscut each step, then rip away the waste.

With my contractor, Scott Wells, I started the job by making a full-scale drawing of the brackets on ¼-in. hardboard. We then cut out templates for each of the three components: brace, post, and beam.

Cutting the parts

With the stock milled, the next step was to cut the miters for the braces on the miter saw, then to nip off the long point of each miter so that it would be square and perpendicular to the post and beams. We cut the chamfers on the tablesaw with a stop attached to the miter fence.

Next, we used a tablesaw with a dado blade to cut the notches in both ends of each brace. For repetitive work, there's nothing better than making jigs out of your miter-gauge fences. We used the template to dial in the jig and the depth of the dado cut.

We also made a template with two stops, one for the beams and one for the posts, to plunge-rout the dadoes that receive the braces. We used the bandsaw to cut the pillowed steps in the legs.

The time invested in making templates, jigs, and stops really paid off. We were able to cut all the pieces and assemble 20 brackets in no time and didn't make any mistakes. The joinery needed only a slight amount of trimming for minor discrepancies in material thickness.

To make the installation easier for the structural brackets that would support the small gable roofs, we added steel braces to the tops of the arms. Covered by the roof, the brackets didn't need additional flashing. Beam ends that project past the roof are chamfered to drain water.

PUT THE BRACKETS TO WORK

The brackets were bolted to the exterior wall, where they support a small entry roof. The roof timbers are Douglas fir, stained to match the factory-stained bracket stock. A smart flashing detail allows the eventual replacement of the roof shingles without disturbing the siding.

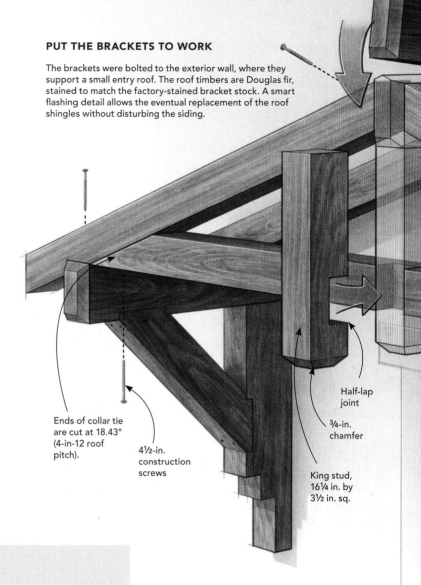

Ends of collar tie
are cut at 18.43°
(4-in-12 roof
pitch).

4½-in.
construction
screws

Half-lap
joint

¾-in.
chamfer

King stud,
16¼ in. by
3½ in. sq.

ASSEMBLE THE BRACKETS IN PLACE

1. After tacking a block to the wall as a rest, mount the post plumb on the wall, securing it with a ½-in. by 6-in. lag screw countersunk in the mortise and driven into 4x4 blocking installed in the walls at the framing stage.
2. Fasten the brace into mortises with 4½-in. construction screws.
3. Attach the beam to the post with a ½-in. by 12-in. lag screw, countersunk into the mortise meant for a steel brace.
4. Screw the brace to the wall and to the top of the bracket.

1

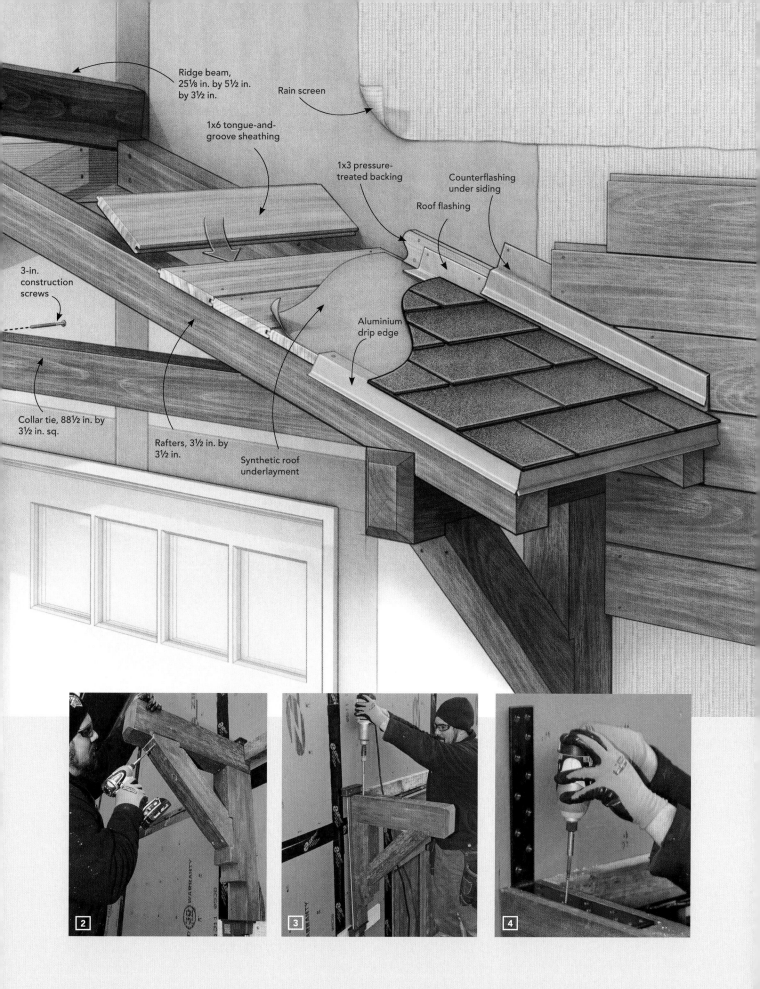

Ridge beam,
25⅛ in. by 5½ in.
by 3½ in.

Rain screen

1x6 tongue-and-
groove sheathing

1x3 pressure-
treated backing

Counterflashing
under siding

Roof flashing

3-in.
construction
screws

Aluminium
drip edge

Collar tie, 88½ in. by
3½ in. sq.

Rafters, 3½ in. by
3½ in.

Synthetic roof
underlayment

Collar and Rafter Ties

BY DEBRA JUDGE SILBER

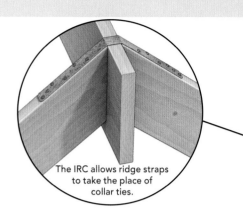

The IRC allows ridge straps to take the place of collar ties.

Builders have been installing collar ties for years, and for years, space-starved home-owners have been asking to have them removed. The proper thing to do, of course, hinges on knowing why they're there in the first place.

Contrary to popular belief, collar ties are not there to support rafters or to keep walls below from spreading under the weight of the roof. That's the job of the rafter ties or the ceiling joists.

Located in the bottom third of the roof structure, rafter ties effectively resist the horizontal forces caused by gravity loads that would otherwise cause the roof to pancake, pushing the sidewalls out. Rafter ties (or ceiling joists acting as rafter ties) are required by code unless the house is designed so that the walls or a structural ridge beam carries the full load of the roof.

Installed in the top third of the roof structure, collar ties prevent separation of the roof at the ridge due to wind uplift.

Here's how collar ties and rafter ties work.

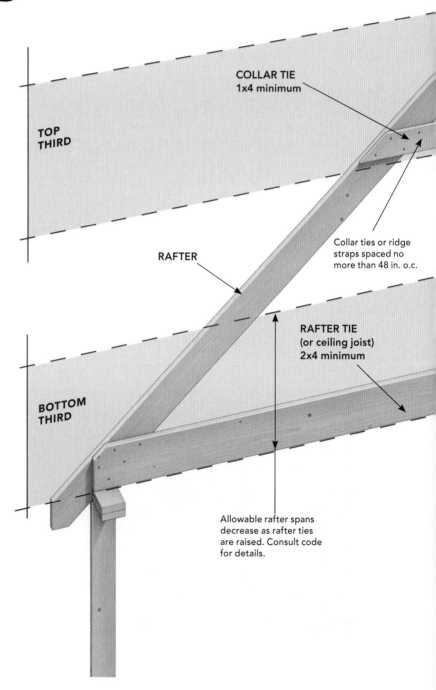

TOP THIRD

COLLAR TIE
1x4 minimum

RAFTER

Collar ties or ridge straps spaced no more than 48 in. o.c.

BOTTOM THIRD

RAFTER TIE
(or ceiling joist)
2x4 minimum

Allowable rafter spans decrease as rafter ties are raised. Consult code for details.

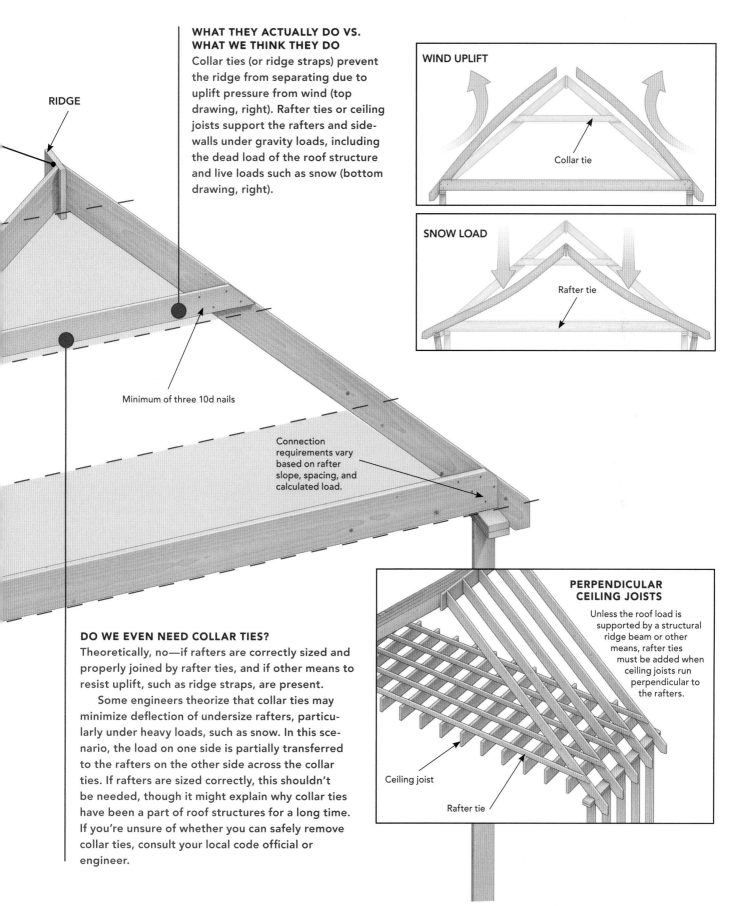

WHAT THEY ACTUALLY DO VS. WHAT WE THINK THEY DO

Collar ties (or ridge straps) prevent the ridge from separating due to uplift pressure from wind (top drawing, right). Rafter ties or ceiling joists support the rafters and sidewalls under gravity loads, including the dead load of the roof structure and live loads such as snow (bottom drawing, right).

RIDGE

Minimum of three 10d nails

Connection requirements vary based on rafter slope, spacing, and calculated load.

WIND UPLIFT

Collar tie

SNOW LOAD

Rafter tie

DO WE EVEN NEED COLLAR TIES?

Theoretically, no—if rafters are correctly sized and properly joined by rafter ties, and if other means to resist uplift, such as ridge straps, are present.

Some engineers theorize that collar ties may minimize deflection of undersize rafters, particularly under heavy loads, such as snow. In this scenario, the load on one side is partially transferred to the rafters on the other side across the collar ties. If rafters are sized correctly, this shouldn't be needed, though it might explain why collar ties have been a part of roof structures for a long time. If you're unsure of whether you can safely remove collar ties, consult your local code official or engineer.

PERPENDICULAR CEILING JOISTS

Unless the roof load is supported by a structural ridge beam or other means, rafter ties must be added when ceiling joists run perpendicular to the rafters.

Ceiling joist

Rafter tie

Framing an Octagonal Turret Roof

BY RICK ARNOLD

The first time I saw an octagonal turret on a set of plans, I cringed. I knew that if I tried to fake my way through framing it with strings and T-bevels, I would lose money in both labor and material, so I decided to do some research first. After looking through a couple of old timber-framing books at the library (this was before the Internet), I discovered that it wasn't that difficult to understand. In fact, the octagonal turret is simply a continuation of a 45° bay-window roof, which I had successfully built many times.

Since then, I haven't really changed my basic approach to framing an octagonal turret, but I have streamlined a few procedures that eliminate the cringe factor. First, I figure out the framing dimensions with a calculator. Then I cut all the parts and assemble the roof on the deck, next to its intended location.

AN OCTAGONAL PLAN
In this example, the octagon segments are 4 ft. long and combine to create a base width of 9 ft. 7⅞ in. A total of eight common and eight hip rafters make a roof with a 20-in-12 pitch.

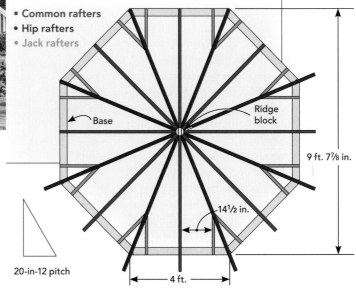

- **Common rafters**
- **Hip rafters**
- Jack rafters

Base

Ridge block

9 ft. 7⅞ in.

14½ in.

20-in-12 pitch

4 ft.

FIND THE COMMON-RAFTER LENGTH as you would for a conventional roof. First, determine the adjusted run by dividing the footprint of the roof in half; then subtract half the thickness of the ridge. (See ridge detail, right.)

CALCULATE THE COMMON-RAFTER LENGTH

Turret-base width: 9 ft. 7⅞ in. ÷ 2 = 4 ft. 9¹⁵/₁₆ in.
Adjusted run: half the turret base (4 ft. 9¹⁵/₁₆ in.) minus half the ridge (1⅞ in.) = 4 ft. 8¹/₁₆ in.

Using a construction calculator:

Enter 4 ft. 8¹/₁₆ in., then PRESS Run .

Enter 20 in., then PRESS Pitch .

PRESS Diag . The common rafter length = 9 ft. ¹⁵/₁₆ in.

PRESS Rise = 7 ft. 9⁷/₁₆ in. (record the rise for calculating the hip rafter).

RIDGE DETAIL. Three pieces of 2x stock cut a couple of inches longer than the hip plumb cut are ripped and beveled to form the octagonal ridge block that measures 3¾ in. square.

OVERLAPPING DOUBLE PLATES GIVE THE BASE GREATER STRENGTH. When complete, the base is blocked up so that the rafters with tails can be installed.

Plan first, cut rafters, then assemble the base

After drawing the plan and figuring out the various framing lengths and angles, I pick the best stock for one common rafter to use as a pattern for the rest. Then I start building the base. I like to build the entire turret on the deck near where it will be located, but away from the edge so that my crew can frame, sheathe, and roof the entire structure without staging or extension ladders.

HIP RAFTERS: BEVEL THE PLUMB CUTS AND ADJUST THE BIRD'S MOUTHS

TO CALCULATE THE HIP RAFTER, use the triangle formed by the adjusted common-rafter run, the adjusted hip-rafter run, and the connecting exterior-wall segment (all in plan view, as if you were calculating floor joists) to determine the length of the adjusted hip-rafter run. Use the known angle formed by the common and hip runs in the center of an octagon, which is always 22.5°.

CALCULATE THE HIP-RAFTER LENGTH

Enter adjusted common run (4 ft. 8$\frac{1}{16}$ in.), then PRESS Run .

Enter 22.5, then PRESS Pitch .

PRESS Diag to get the adjusted hip run, 5 ft. $\frac{11}{16}$ in.

Enter adjusted hip run (5 ft. $\frac{11}{16}$ in.), then PRESS Run .

Enter common-rafter rise (7 ft. 9$\frac{7}{16}$ in.), then PRESS Rise .

PRESS Diag to get the hip-rafter length (9 ft. 3$\frac{7}{16}$ in.).

CALCULATE THE HIP DROP

To mark the hips' bird's mouths, slide the framing square along the plumb line until the HAP (height above plate) reads the same as the common rafter. The hip rafter must be lowered or its edges will be above the plane of the sheathing. The determining factor in dropping the hip is the thickness of that rafter. Instead of cutting a double bevel (also called backing) along the hip's top edge, it's easier to calculate the drop and subtract that amount from the HAP.

Enter 67.5, then PRESS Pitch .

Enter half the thickness of the rafter (¾ in.). PRESS Rise .

PRESS Run = $\frac{5}{16}$ in.

Pitch (20) x run ($\frac{5}{16}$ in.) = 6$\frac{3}{16}$ in.

Divide by unit run of an octagon hip:
6$\frac{3}{16}$ in. ÷ 12.9887 = ½ in. drop.

½-in. drop

Hip's bird's mouth

7$\frac{7}{16}$-in. height above plate (HAP)

Common's bird's mouth

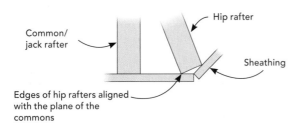

Common/jack rafter

Hip rafter

Sheathing

Edges of hip rafters aligned with the plane of the commons

BEVEL SOLUTIONS. The double bevel for the top plumb cut is 67.5°. Because most saws don't swing much past 45°, draw a centerline along the length of the square plumb cut. Then set the bevel at 22.5°, and cut in both directions along that centerline.

ADD A PAIR OF JACKS TO EACH HIP

BECAUSE THE OCTAGON WALLS ARE ONLY 4 ft. long, there will be only two jack rafters per wall. With the jacks laid out from each side of the common rafter, both (and therefore all) jack rafters will be the same length, but with opposite cheek cuts. By adjusting the same plan-view triangle used to calculate the run of the hip, you can determine the run of the jack.

Enter 14½ in., then PRESS $\boxed{\text{Rise}}$.

Enter 22.5, then PRESS $\boxed{\text{Pitch}}$.

PRESS $\boxed{\text{Run}}$ to get 35 in.

To calculate the jack run, subtract run (35 in.) from adjusted run (4 ft. 8¹⁄₁₆ in.) to equal 1 ft. 9¹⁄₁₆ in. However, you still need to account for the thickness of the hip rafter so that the jack layout remains true.

ACCOUNT FOR THE THICKNESS OF THE HIP RAFTER

Enter one-half the thickness of the rafter (¾ in.), then PRESS $\boxed{\text{Run}}$.

Enter pitch (67.5), then PRESS $\boxed{\text{Pitch}}$.

PRESS $\boxed{\text{Diag}}$ = 1¹⁵⁄₁₆ in.

Jack run (1 ft. 9¹⁄₁₆ in.) minus 1¹⁵⁄₁₆ in. = 1 ft. 7⅛ in.

Enter 1 ft. 7⅛ in., then PRESS $\boxed{\text{Run}}$.

Enter 20 in., then PRESS $\boxed{\text{Pitch}}$.

PRESS $\boxed{\text{Diag}}$ = 3 ft. 1³⁄₁₆ in. for the jack-rafter length.

CHEEK CUT. Use a Big Foot saw to cut the cheek on the jack rafter.

The first step is to snap the turret-wall outline on the third-floor deck. I plan for double top plates so that I can overlap them at the corners, which helps to stabilize the structure as I build on it.

Once the walls are built, I block them up off the floor to make room for the rafter tails that, when in place, will extend past the floor deck to meet the fascia of the regular roof. Then I recheck and adjust the octagon until its measurements are exact.

Assemble the rafters

I make the ridge from three pieces of 2x6 stock cut a bit longer than the length of the hip plumb cut. The center piece is ripped at 3¾ in. The sides are ripped at 3¾ in. by 1⅛ in., then beveled at a 45° angle. I nail a pair of opposing common rafters to the ridge, then swing the ridge up and fasten it into position. Then I add the remaining six commons, followed by the hip rafters and jacks.

Because the roof sections are so small, there is little tolerance for out-of-plane members, so I check with a straightedge. If there's a significant problem, I even it out with a cordless planer. When all the rafters and the fascia are in place, my crew and I nail on most of the sheathing, leaving a place for access from inside the third floor. We shingle as much as possible while the structure is still on the deck, which saves a considerable amount of labor and is much safer than doing it from staging. After completing as much work as possible, the whole crew gets underneath the turret and walks it into place. After removing the blocking, we nail the turret base to the deck and start to fill in the rest of the roof.

GET IT NEARLY FINISHED, THEN SLIDE IT IN PLACE. Except for the portion that will be enclosed by the roof, the turret is sheathed and shingled on the deck. With most of the crew lifting from inside, the turret roof is moved to its location on the exterior wall. Once in place, the blocks are removed and the plates can be nailed down.

THE BIG FOOT

A big saw helps to cut the jack rafters, which are marked exactly like a shorter common rafter. The tricky part comes in the cheek cut. Here, I use the same method of setting a saw's bevel to 22.5°, but I pull out the Big Foot saw to make the cut. A true production saw, its 10¼-in. blade increases the cutting depth to nearly 4 in. at that angle to make almost an entire bevel cut. (Here, I still had to finish the cut with a handsaw or reciprocating saw.) Manufactured by Big Foot Tools, the saw isn't cheap. It retails for around $420, but Big Foot also makes saw-conversion kits (about $300) that turn worm-drive saws into big-capacity saws.

Framing a Classic Shed Dormer

BY JOHN SPIER

O f all the ways to bump out a roof, I think shed dormers offer the most bang for the buck. They're easy to build, are simple to finish, and provide lots of usable interior space. So why aren't all dormers sheds? Compared to dog-house, eyebrow, or A-frame dormers, shed dormers aren't always the prettiest option. On the back side of a house, though, beauty sometimes needs to take a backseat to utility. Besides, with some attention to size, shape, and proportion, a shed dormer can actually look pretty good.

Unfortunately, many builders don't take the time to think about the details before they get started working on a shed-dormer project. Many years of building have taught me that if I spend a little extra time planning a shed dormer, then I spend a lot less time trying to make a bunch of mistakes look good later.

SAFETY NOTE. Although John feels comfortable working on the scaffolding shown here, in this situation OSHA guidelines call for the use of guardrails, a safety net, or a personal fall-arrest system.

DORMER DESIGN SHOULD BE PRACTICAL AND PLEASING TO THE EYE

IT'S HARD TO MAKE A POORLY planned dormer look good, so it's crucial to consider the relationship between design and construction at every step of the project. Beginning with chalklines that represent the gable ends, I like to create a full-size section of the dormer right on the subfloor so that I can work out all the important details before I begin framing.

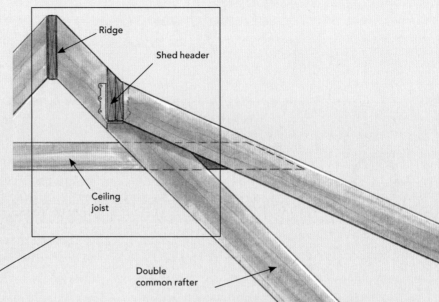

Ridge

Shed header

Ceiling joist

Double common rafter

1. ROOF PITCH

First and foremost, it's important—both functionally and visually—to maintain adequate roof pitch on a shed dormer. Steeper almost always looks better, and the steeper the main roof, the steeper the dormer should be. I regard a pitch of 4-in-12 as a minimum, not least because this is the practical minimum for installing conventional roofing materials such as asphalt or cedar shingles. Keep in mind, though, that a 4-in-12 dormer might look good on an 8-in-12 roof, but a 10-in-12 or 12-in-12 roof needs a steeper shed to look right.

When it comes time to build, you can meet a specific pitch by using a calculator, or you can use the full-size sub-floor drawing to decide on the appropriate pitch. Either way you work it, the pitch could need some tweaking to look right. The two most important things to consider are the height of the front wall and the location where the tops of the rafters meet the main roof. Shed dormers that share the ridge with the main roof (see below) are the easiest to build, but smaller dormers look better with their roofs intersecting lower. Keep in mind that close to the ridge but not connected isn't good. If the dormer doesn't peak at the ridge, you need to leave adequate room for roof vents and flashing.

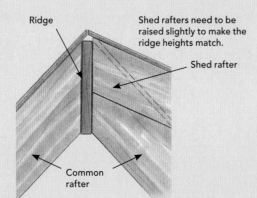

Ridge

Shed rafters need to be raised slightly to make the ridge heights match.

Shed rafter

Common rafter

Alternative: Dormers that peak at the ridge

Shed dormers that peak at the ridge are easier to frame, but be careful of the intersection of the two differing roof pitches. If you align the tops of the dormer rafters with the tops of the common rafters, the difference in roof pitches will lead to finished ridge heights that don't match. Raising the shed rafter slightly solves the problem.

2. OVERHANGS AND HEADER HEIGHT

Dormer-roof trim and eave overhangs typically mimic the main roof, though scaling down the sizes is usually appropriate. Whatever the desired look, the details should be worked out at the framing stage. I draw in the window headers, figure the overhang, and draw out every layer from subfascia to finished trim. In conventional 8-ft.-high walls, window heads are typically between 80 in. to 84 in. from the floor. This height provides comfortable viewing for most people in a standing position and also aligns window tops with door tops. In a shed dormer, though, ceiling heights are often reduced, so it's acceptable to lower the window heights as well. Whenever possible, I raise the window headers a bit (drawing right). This gives me the option of increasing the size of the windows if the design dictates.

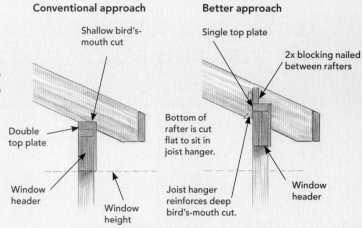

Conventional approach
- Shallow bird's-mouth cut
- Double top plate
- Window header
- Window height

Better approach
- Single top plate
- 2x blocking nailed between rafters
- Bottom of rafter is cut flat to sit in joist hanger.
- Joist hanger reinforces deep bird's-mouth cut.
- Window header

A better look: Raise the height of windows

This often-seen and, in my opinion, always ugly detail (above, left) has become the conventional approach to building the front edge of the dormer roof. It's easy to frame, but it forces you to lower the windows to accommodate the header. But by cutting a deep bird's mouth in the shed rafter and capping the wall with a single top plate, I can move up the header and raise the window height.

3. WINDOWS AND TRIM

Just as the proportions of the dormer should relate to the main roof, so should the proportions of the windows relate to the front wall of the dormer. It's often helpful to use horizontally proportioned windows, which in many cases actually complement a well-designed shed dormer. But take extra time planning the trim details below the windows; this is a notorious trouble spot and is difficult to correct without seeming like an afterthought. The only sure way I've found to get the spacing correct is to draw the trim components on the full-size subfloor plans. Ideally, the windowsills either should land just above the roofing or should be raised up the height of one course of siding or trim. Anywhere between leaves an awkward course of siding or affects the trim proportions.

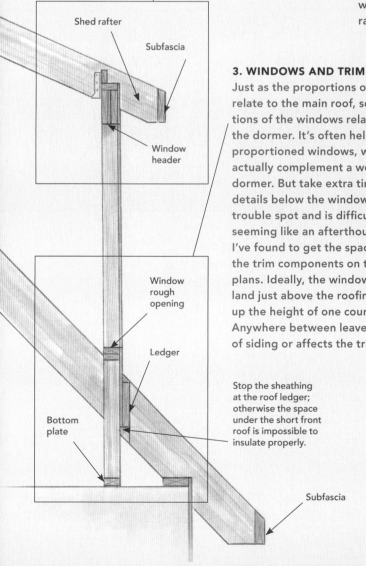

- Shed rafter
- Subfascia
- Window header
- Window rough opening
- Ledger
- Bottom plate
- Subfascia

Stop the sheathing at the roof ledger; otherwise the space under the short front roof is impossible to insulate properly.

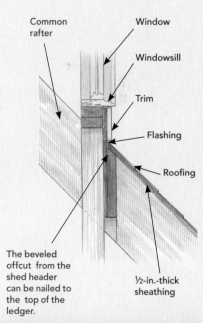

- Common rafter
- Window
- Windowsill
- Trim
- Flashing
- Roofing
- The beveled offcut from the shed header can be nailed to the top of the ledger.
- ½-in.-thick sheathing

RAISE THE WALL, BUT NOT QUITE PLUMB. Unless ceiling joists will bear directly on the top plate of the front wall, I like to lean the wall in about ⅛ in. before bracing it; the rafter loads will push the wall out as the building settles and the crowns on the rafters flatten.

SOLID PLANNING PAYS OFF AT THE BUILDING STAGE

WITH A LITTLE EXTRA PLANNING, all the dormer components fit together nicely on the first try. For instance, the full-size drawing made it obvious that to ensure a smooth transition between the two different planes of roof sheathing, the dormer rafters (inset photo) should be cut so that they sit just below the beveled dormer head.

1. SHEATHE THE CHEEK WALLS BEFORE THE ROOF

Always sheathe the cheek walls before you sheathe the roof; it's a lot easier to trace these oddly shaped pieces than it is to measure and fit them. Just remember to cut the wall sheathing ¼ in. short. If scribed to the top and cut exactly, the wall sheathing will push up on the roof sheathing as the rafters dry and shrink.

2. SHORT RAFTERS FROM THE COMMON-RAFTER TEMPLATE

The short rafters that make up the small piece of roof in front of the shed dormer can be traced from the same template used to make the common rafters; you just need to adjust the location of the plumb cut. Don't forget to subtract the thickness of the beveled ledger from the rafter length before making the cuts. Toenail these rafters to the bottom plate running along the outside edge of the subfloor; then nail them to the ledger on the face of the wall.

3. A CHALKLINE GUIDES CEILING-JOIST PLACEMENT

If the ceiling will flatten at the peak, it's crucial to keep the joists in plane with each other so that the joint between the ceiling and the dormer roof is straight, and so that the ceiling remains flat. I start by measuring the ceiling height up from the subfloor at all four corners of the room; then I snap a chalkline between the points and install the joists with their bottom edge on the chalkline.

The subfloor becomes a big set of blueprints

There are as many ways to frame shed dormers as there are ways to design them. The dormer featured here doesn't peak at the ridge the way that many shed dormers do, but the lessons here can be applied to shed dormers of all kinds, new construction or remodel.

Whenever possible, I take details from the framing plans and re-create them full size on the subfloor. I start by snapping chalklines on the subfloor to represent the gable end. After building and standing these walls, I snap more chalklines to complete the full-scale section drawing of the rest of the roof.

Next, I draw the ridge, and if there will be a header for the dormer, I draw that, too. At this point, I can lay out the dormer rafters and then snap the lines for them. This part of the drawing can be worked in either direction: If I have a specified or desired pitch, I get out my calculator and then figure out where to draw the rafter. Otherwise, I follow some rules of thumb for shed-dormer rafters and then use the calculator to figure out what the roof pitch really is (see "Dormer design should be practical and pleasing to the eye," pp. 188–189). Either way, this method allows me to tweak the dormer design before any of the nails are driven.

At this point, I also go as far as to sketch in the thicknesses of the sheathing, the roofing, and the flashing. I draw all the trim details full scale so that I know they will fit and look right. Sometimes I play around with the drawing until I'm satisfied, then draw a clean version on the other end of the floor for reference. The process might sound time-consuming, but it pays big dividends later.

Building is the easy part

Once all the thinking and figuring are done, building a shed dormer is easy. I start with the front wall of the dormer. I build it flat on the subfloor, sheathe it, apply housewrap, and stand it like any other wall. When the front wall is stood, I brace the ends, run a stringline, and straighten it with some intermediate braces. Next, I build the short roof in front of the dormer, though this step can just as easily be done later if you prefer.

The layout for the dormer rafters can be taken from the drawing on the subfloor, but I often cheat by making the plumb cut at the top and holding the rafter in place to mark the bird's mouth and tail cuts. Whichever way you do it, make a pattern rafter, and test it at both ends of the front wall and in the middle before you cut and hang the rafters.

Cheek walls on each end of the shed dormer can be done three ways: framed in place and extending all the way up, framed flat to the ceiling and crippled in above, or framed only from the common rafter to the dormer roof for an open plan. Always sheathe these walls before the roof, though; it's easier to trace these oddly shaped pieces than it is to measure and fit them. Just remember to cut the sheathing ¼ in. shy to allow for rafter shrinkage. I finish by building the rake overhangs and adding the subfascia, the blocking, the hardware, and the sheathing.

CHEEK WALLS ARE FRAMED IN PLACE

START THE CHEEK WALLS BY NAILING a top plate along the underside of the outer-most shed rafter. Next, cut the bottom plate to the desired length, slide it against a previously framed wall to lay out the stud spacing quickly (1), and nail the plate to the subfloor. Use a level to plumb up from each stud mark on the bottom plate, then measure the length, cut the studs with the appropriate top angle, and toenail in place (2). Finish the cheek walls by nailing angled blocking to the doubled rafters at each stud bay (3). The blocking should extend past the top of the rafter to provide solid nailing for the cheek-wall sheathing.

Three Ways to Lay Out an Elliptical Curve

BY JUD PEAKE

As defined by *Merriam-Webster's Collegiate Dictionary*, an ellipse is "a closed plane curve generated by a point moving in such a way that the sums of its distances from two fixed points [foci] is a constant; a plane section of a right circular cone that is a closed curve." Got it? Luckily, it's a lot easier to see an ellipse than to understand its definition. Just cut a dowel to 90° at one end and to 45° at the other. The square cut creates a circle with a uniform radius as wide as it is tall. The 45° cut end reveals an ellipse, wider than it is tall.

This ellipse is an example of the geometry of some larger building components. Because these curves are quantifiable, their rise and run can be deter-

A ROOF OF CURVES PROVES THE TECHNIQUE. As part of the crew working on the restoration of the Conservatory of Flowers in San Francisco, the author was able to refine his ability to create elliptical rafters.

mined using the conventions of roof framing. For instance, a cove ceiling with a common section that is a simple 12-in. quarter radius would have a corner strut or hip that is a quarter ellipse with a rise of 12 in. and a run of 17 in.

There are several ways to lay out an ellipse. Here, I'll describe three using that 12:17 rise: run ratio. The first is the string method, which is the most familiar. Use string that won't stretch, although longer lengths of string tend to stretch, no matter what. The string length can be found by formula, but sometimes it's simpler just to pull a string around the two foci and to a known point on the curve, such as, in this example, up 12 in. on the minor axis.

The second technique, which is derived straight from the determined rise and run, is to use a trammel. The trammel rides around the square corner of a piece of plywood or other suitable material. The trammel-drawn curve (right) gives the correct ellipse for a regular hip on a 12-in. radial cove ceiling or curved-rafter roof. To draw a hip on an octagonal roof, the trammel is set up with a 12-in. rise and 13-in. run.

The third is an arithmetic plotting, also known as lofting, which can also be applied to any curve. This method comes in handy when you need to derive a hip or valley from an existing, unquantified curve, or if the ellipse is too big to draw with a trammel. During the restoration of San Francisco's Conservatory of Flowers (photos, p. 193), both scenarios were true. We drew a grid of 12-in. squares on the floor and then calculated the shape of the curved com-

mon rafters, hips, and valleys. Once the hips and valleys were cut to shape, we cut the backing with a changing double bevel that began as two 45° cuts at the bottom plumb end of the curve and diminished to a single flat edge at the top, level end.

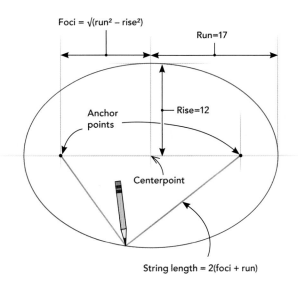

Foci = $\sqrt{(run^2 - rise^2)}$

Run=17

Rise=12

Anchor points

Centerpoint

String length = 2(foci + run)

1 USE A STRING

Draw an ellipse with a string, two pins, and a pencil. First, draw a horizontal line and mark a centerpoint. Next, determine the rise and run of the ellipse. The string's anchor points, called the foci, are located with the following equation: foci = $\sqrt{(run^2 - rise^2)}$. The string length can be calculated this way: string length = 2(foci + run). After finding the centerpoint and foci, attach a nonstretching string of the correct length to nails or screws driven in at the foci. Using the string to restrain the pencil, draw the ellipse.

WHAT IS AN ELLIPSE?

THE END OF A SQUARE-CUT DOWEL IS A CIRCLE, in which the rise (height) and the run (width) are the same, resulting in a uniform radius. But cut the dowel at 45°, and the end is an ellipse, which is wider than it is high. Its radius is variable.

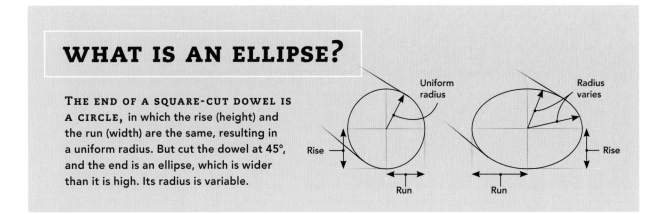

Uniform radius

Radius varies

Rise

Rise

Run

Run

2 USE A STICK

Drill a hole for a pencil in the middle of a 1x2. From the pencil's centerline, measure the distance of the desired rise (the y coordinate) of the ellipse (for example, 12 in.), and drive a screw or nail through the trammel. In the opposite direction, measure the distance of the run (the x coordinate; 17 in., for example), and set another screw or nail. (For accuracy, the pins should be just outside the measured point.) To draw the ellipse, align the pins and pencil along the vertical edge of the work-piece. While keeping the pins tight to the plywood edges, move the bottom pin (the rise) to the right as the top pin (the run) descends the vertical.

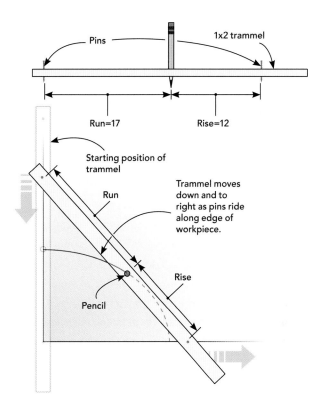

3 USE A GRID

If an ellipse is too big to lay out with a trammel, it can be drawn using an algebraic formula. Begin by drawing a grid on an appropriately sized piece of paper, a sheet of plywood, or the subfloor. If you divide the horizontal axis into 20 parts, you'll be plenty accurate. To draw the companion hip or valley to a curved common rafter, you'll want first to draw the common. For the sake of illustration, we'll use a quarter radius to describe the common, which can be drawn by swinging an arc from the intersection of the x axis and y axis. The elliptical hip or valley is laid out as an extension of the common, in a ratio of 12:17. On the grid, although each unit of rise remains the same, every 12 in. of run gets stretched to 17 in. to describe regular hips or valleys. To elongate the radius into an ellipse, multiply each point on the x axis (which represents the run) by the square root of 2, which is 1.414. The y axis (representing the rise) stays the same.

After the coordinates are laid out, tack a flexible strip of wood at each point of the stretched grid to describe the elongated curved line. Now the ellipse can be transferred onto the stock.

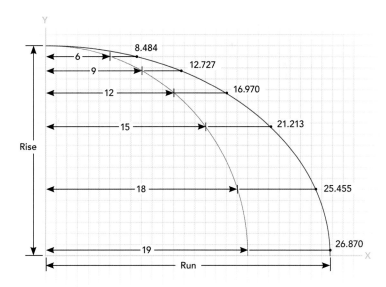

To plot an elliptical curve with a ratio of 12:17, multiply points along the horizontal axis that intersect the radius by the square root of 2, which is 1.414. **Example:** 1.414 x 6 = 8.484

Roof Trusses

BY ROB MUNACH

Dead loads

The weight of the roof, the truss itself, attic insulation, floor sheathing, ductwork, and drywall used for the ceiling.

Top chord

Supports the dead load of the materials used to construct the roof, the live load of workers building or maintaining the roof, and wind and snow loads.

Bottom chord

Supports the dead load of ceiling materials and the live loads of homeowners accessing the attic as well as the weight of the items stored in the attic. The bottom chord also serves as a rafter tie and keeps the top of the exterior walls from thrusting outward.

Web

Helps to support and to transfer the compression and tension forces from one chord to the other. Individually, the web members also are in tension and compression, depending on their location in the truss and the direction of the loads on the truss.

Nail plates

Components are fastened together with toothed metal plates that are machine-pressed to the members.

-418

-1696

1535

A roof truss is an engineered building component designed to span longer distances than dimensional lumber without relying on interior partition walls for support. The most common truss, a 2x4 Fink truss, is designed to support several different loads. On pp. 198–204, Paul Johnson and Nathan D. Young show how to build complex roofs with trusses. Whether you're framing a new roof or remodeling an existing truss roof, it's important to know what components make up a truss and how it works.

Better bracing

Nailing 2x4 T-bracing to the top edge of long web members prevents them from deflecting sideways. T-bracing takes more time to install than continuous lateral bracing and is more expensive, but it's more effective and easier to install correctly.

Continuous lateral bracing

T-bracing

TRUSS PERFORMANCE BY THE NUMBERS

In a truss, the bottom chord and the top chord are under tension and compression forces as a result of the loads on the roof. Which chord carries tension and which carries compression depends on the direction of the overall loading on the truss. The loads on the truss are generally in a downward direction, but may turn upward during extreme wind. The numbers below are the actual compression and tension ratings of a truss that has been modeled with a combined dead, live, and snow load of 40 lb. per sq. ft. They illustrate the push-pull relationships of all the truss members.

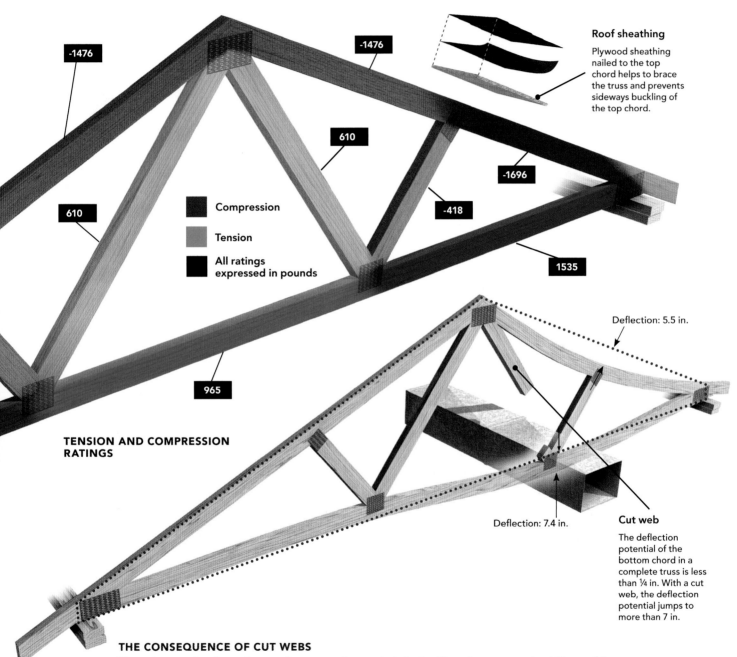

Roof sheathing

Plywood sheathing nailed to the top chord helps to brace the truss and prevents sideways buckling of the top chord.

-1476

-1476

-1696

610

610

-418

1535

Compression

Tension

All ratings expressed in pounds

965

TENSION AND COMPRESSION RATINGS

Deflection: 5.5 in.

Deflection: 7.4 in.

Cut web

The deflection potential of the bottom chord in a complete truss is less than ¼ in. With a cut web, the deflection potential jumps to more than 7 in.

THE CONSEQUENCE OF CUT WEBS

There is no redundancy in a roof truss, and as such, it is significantly compromised if any of its members are cut or damaged. Unfortunately, it is common to see trusses that have had webs and chords cut to accommodate attic access, skylights, or HVAC ductwork. A few cut trusses don't necessarily lead to catastrophic roof failure, because the roof acts like a large diaphragm and because partition walls below usually pick up some of the roof loads. However, the deflection that can occur when truss members are incorrectly altered can be substantial, which can lead to damage of interior finishes and materials.

Framing Tricky Truss Roofs

BY PAUL JOHNSON AND
NATHAN D. YOUNG

I t's estimated that nearly 80% of the roofs on new houses are framed with trusses rather than conventional rafters. The reason for this is simple: Roof trusses are faster to install, which lowers labor costs and results in quicker occupancy. In seismically active areas, such as the Pacific Northwest region where we build, using trusses is generally the simplest way to build a complex roof that satisfies code and local inspectors. It has also been our experience that perhaps one framing crew in a dozen

could efficiently stick-frame the complicated roof of a custom home like the one shown here.

On this job, the architect sent his detailed roof plan to the truss company, which used computer software to design the individual trusses and to plan the layout. Once the foundation was in place, a representative from the truss company checked the site for factors that would complicate delivery and took final measurements of the foundation. The truss package was delivered 10 days later.

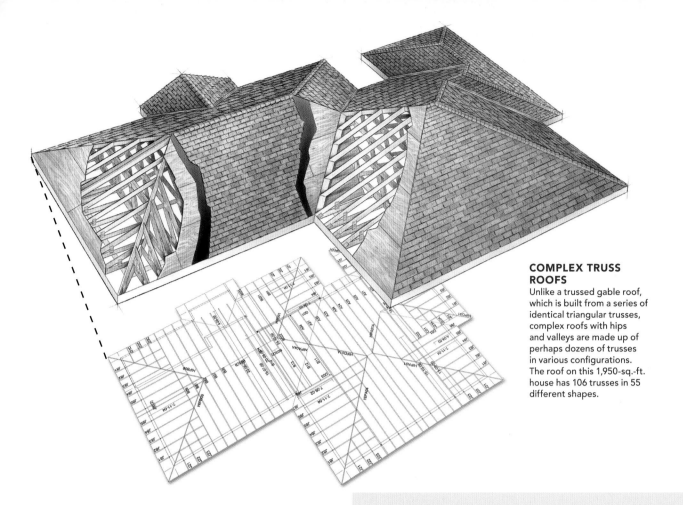

COMPLEX TRUSS ROOFS
Unlike a trussed gable roof, which is built from a series of identical triangular trusses, complex roofs with hips and valleys are made up of perhaps dozens of trusses in various configurations. The roof on this 1,950-sq.-ft. house has 106 trusses in 55 different shapes.

Make a plan for delivery

Depending on their length, trusses may arrive on a flatbed truck that has an onboard crane, or they may be delivered on a semi and unloaded with a separate crane. On this project, they came on a 60-plus-ft. flatbed with an onboard crane. Even with this big truck, the trusses still stuck out the back by 10 ft., which meant that the truck was blocking a lane in the street. Further complicating matters, the truck driver, who was also the crane operator, had to navigate around trees to get the trusses off the truck, which prolonged the delivery process.

It wasn't a problem on this job, but the parking area for the truck needs to be wide enough to accommodate the stabilizers for the crane. Because the truck is heavy, the truss company may require a damage waiver to protect it from lawsuits if the truck breaks a paved driveway. We often use scraps of LVLs under the stabilizers to help spread the load when the truck is on concrete or asphalt.

STICK WITH THE PLAN

PERHAPS THE MOST IMPORTANT ELEMENT IN framing a truss roof is the plan provided by the truss manufacturer. It identifies every truss and truss location with a three- or four-digit code. A paper label attached to the truss corresponds with the coding on the plan. The plan is so important that Portland-area truss manufacturers laminate the drawing so that it can stand up to the area's notoriously wet weather. Plan in hand, the framer decides where to start and in what order he'll lift and set the trusses.

LAYOUT COMES FIRST. With a three-person crew, the lead carpenter lays out a section of roof and then gets the other two framers started on setting the trusses. Once things are moving along, he starts laying out the next section of roof. It's a good idea to figure out where you'll set the truss bundles so that you don't have to move them later.

WHEN POSSIBLE, LIFT SETS. A group of banded trusses is stronger and less prone to damaging flex than are individual trusses. Too much flex will cause a truss's steel gussets to pop off, destroying the truss.

The truss company is responsible for getting the trusses to the job and will set the bundled trusses on the ground, or on the wall plates if they can reach, but they won't spend the time to set individual trusses. On most residential projects, this isn't a problem, but on commercial and large residential jobs with especially long or tall spans, it's worth the cost of hiring a crane to set individual trusses while the framers brace them (see "Framing with a Crane," pp. 70–76). We've also been on jobs where the delivery truck can't get the trusses on the roof because of their size or because of poor access. In these situations, we bring in a smaller crane or an all-terrain forklift to lift trusses individually or in bundles.

Precise layout and understanding of the truss plan is the key to making a truss roof with hips and valleys that come together. A good truss manufacturer provides a detailed layout, bracing instructions, and all the necessary hardware. However, you'll need a basic understanding of roof framing for the plan to make sense. Fortunately, truss and stick-frame roofs share much of the same terminology.

Where do you start?

The first step is to look critically at the plan and decide which truss to place first. It usually makes sense to start with a girder truss in one of the hip or valley sections of the roof. As their name suggests, girder trusses support other trusses, and they're common on complex truss roofs. We start with a girder truss because once the girder truss is fastened to the other trusses that it helps to support, these assemblies are sturdy and largely self-bracing. We also find it easier to compensate for irregularities in the layout by adjusting common trusses rather than girder trusses and the hip and valley trusses that attach to them.

Once we decide where to start, we transfer the layout from the plan to the top plates. We don't do the entire layout at once; instead, we do it in sections. With a three-person crew, we find it's most efficient to have our lead carpenter start the other two crew members setting trusses in one section. Once things are under way, he continues on the next section of roof. Any of the crew members can direct the crane operator when he's setting the individual or bundled trusses that they're currently working on, but the lead guy is responsible for deciding where to place the bundled trusses that will be installed after the crane leaves.

START WITH THE GIRDERS. Girder trusses almost always have hangers that carry other trusses. It's easier and faster to install the hangers when the truss is lying flat.

Given the high loads imposed on them, girder trusses are often made from multiple truss layers called plies. Many times, the truss company assembles multi-ply trusses, which generally saves time and effort, but it makes sense to leave the plies separate when a multi-ply truss would be too heavy or awkward to set. If you field-assemble multi-ply trusses, follow the manufacturer's fastening schedule. Once a girder section is set and braced, we move on to a neighboring section of roof, then set those trusses and brace them to the girder section.

Go with the recommended bracing

Even though the bracing specified on the truss manufacturer's installation guide can seem like overkill, it's always best to go with it in case something goes wrong. High winds and mishaps can cause trusses to fall like dominoes, and there's seldom anything left to salvage afterward.

That said, on residential projects where smaller trusses have greater structural integrity, the most important thing is solid bracing to keep the first truss upright. The rest of the trusses then can be braced to this truss and braced laterally to each other. We also install diagonal bracing every 12 ft. to 16 ft. to add vertical stability. For this project, we set a major girder truss, braced it, and then installed the perpendicular mono (single-slope) trusses that hang from it. This created a strong, self-bracing assembly that subsequent trusses could be safely braced against.

Once the trusses have been set, we often have additional framing to do in the valleys and blocking to install. Our truss supplier provides blocking as part of the package and even cuts holes and covers them with screening for eave blocking on vented roofs. We usually install the blocking as part of the sheathing process. Truss suppliers can make what are called valley sets, which are trusses that decrease in size to match the roof pitch as they ascend the valley, but we generally find that it's easier to stick-frame these small areas rather than to use trusses.

ENSURE THAT TRUSSES ARE IN THE SAME PLANE. Check the height from the top chord to the top plate often. Assuming equal overhangs and a consistent roof pitch, this measurement should be consistent.

CHECK FOR PLUMB. To achieve their designed strength, trusses should be vertical. Use a spirit level to check for plumb.

HIP AND VALLEY TRUSSES

SHEATHE AS SOON AS POSSIBLE. Truss roofs are much stronger once sheathed. Leave a ⅛-in. gap between panels, and space the nails 6 in. on edges and 8 in. in the field.

HIP TRUSSES

Hip trusses can take several regional forms. In their area, the authors most often see California hips (shown in yellow), which have sloping top chords that extend toward the ridge. In other areas, step-down or Midwest hips may be more common. Hip trusses are often combined with girder trusses (shown in green). Girders equipped with hangers help to support jack trusses (shown in orange).

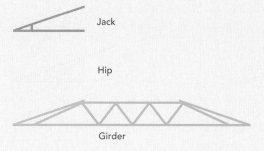

Jack

Hip

Girder

VALLEY TRUSSES

Valleys are usually built with increasingly smaller trusses as they go up the intersecting slope. The authors often find it easier and less expensive to stick-frame these areas after all the trusses are set and the roof is mostly sheathed. The 2x6 site-cut rafters (shown in blue) bear on a 2x8 site-cut "lay board" that runs parallel to the valley center.

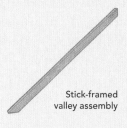

Stick-framed valley assembly

MODIFYING TRUSSES

EVERYTHING YOU READ SAYS NOT TO MODIFY trusses in any way, and for good reason (see "Roof Trusses," pp. 196–197). The truth is, though, that truss companies make mistakes. When this hip truss simply wouldn't fit, it became clear that a worker at the truss company forgot to trim the top chord. After the authors triple-checked that they had the right truss, they decided to cut it themselves. Always inspect carefully what's going on, and discuss anything you're not totally sure about with the truss designer. When a truss is damaged, ask for a repair solution from the truss company. Most things can be fixed with lumber splices or plywood gussets.

The biggest problem occurs in sections with California valleys, where the valley trusses are nailed on top of the sheathing. Manufacturers never seem to compensate for the underlying sheathing, which throws off the layout, so after several attempts, we've decided it's easier to stick-frame these sections ourselves.

We generally use a stringline to locate the ridge board that will receive the rafters. Then, using a construction calculator to find the rafter lengths, we fill in the valley sections with 2x4 or 2x6 rafters nailed to a 2x8 bottom plate that we call a lay board. The calculated rafters are generally close enough that we can scribe them to deal with any inconsistencies. On this complex roof, filling in the valleys took about a day for a skilled framer and one helper.

We start sheathing at the eaves, and then we work up toward the ridge. It's easier to start on large, uninterrupted parts of the roof and then use offcuts for smaller sections. We generally use an all-terrain forklift to get the plywood up to the roof, which is a huge time- and muscle-saver.

Shopping for a truss supplier

The truss package for this 1,950-sq.-ft. house with 2-ft. overhangs cost about $6,500. This included the hip roof for the 450-sq.-ft. garage.

When you're shopping for a truss supplier, ask about the moisture content of the lumber and the truss company's tolerance for wane and crooked stock. When some of the trusses on this job arrived warped and required additional framing to correct, the truss company claimed that 1 in. of deflection is within their standards. We don't think we'll be using them again.

Elegant Eaves for a Truss Roof

BY STEVE BACZEK AND
JIM WOLFFER

Even as we develop more and more standard assemblies for tight, well-insulated building envelopes, there are always some details that require extra thought and ingenuity. Roof overhangs tend to be one of these details. Not only can continuous rafter tails cause a thermal bridge, but they can create a difficult area to air-seal as well. Of course, this all depends on where you locate your air and thermal barriers.

On this single-story, hip-roofed house on Cape Cod, we decided to use the eaves to add some character with exposed cedar rafter tails. Here in New England, eaves are more commonly boxed in with a fascia and soffit. So not only did we have to figure out how not to have this detail be a weak link in the building envelope, but we also had to figure out how to finish the overhang so the homeowners would be looking up at something more pleasing than the underside of the OSB roof sheathing.

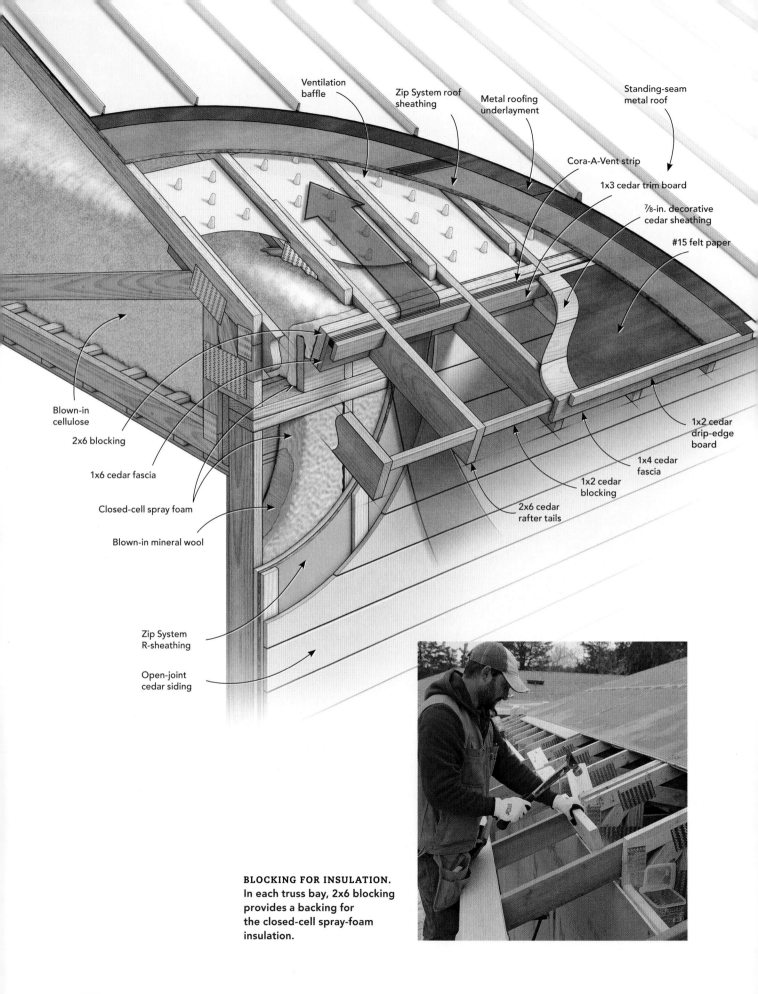

Ventilation baffle

Zip System roof sheathing

Metal roofing underlayment

Standing-seam metal roof

Cora-A-Vent strip

1x3 cedar trim board

⅞-in. decorative cedar sheathing

#15 felt paper

1x2 cedar drip-edge board

1x4 cedar fascia

1x2 cedar blocking

2x6 cedar rafter tails

Blown-in cellulose

2x6 blocking

1x6 cedar fascia

Closed-cell spray foam

Blown-in mineral wool

Zip System R-sheathing

Open-joint cedar siding

BLOCKING FOR INSULATION.
In each truss bay, 2x6 blocking
provides a backing for
the closed-cell spray-foam
insulation.

An energy-smart overhang

With the ability to span long distances, roof trusses are an affordable way to create an open floor plan, but they aren't the best option for an exposed eave detail. In this case, clipped heel trusses are used and the rafter tails are applied. Because the rafter tails are sistered to the trusses, the truss designer had to be aware of the plan in order to offset the layout. The trusses are designed to drop below the wall's top plate inside the house to make room for 24 in. of blown cellulose (R-90) in the ceiling and 12 in. (R-45) at the truss heel above the top plate, and for a vent channel below the roof deck. The Zip System R-sheathing is the primary air barrier on the walls, and the drywall ceiling is the primary air barrier inside, along the ceiling. The two are connected by the top plates and blocking, which are air-sealed with Tremco Acoustical Sealant. The size, length, and nailing pattern of the rafter tails were determined by a structural engineer to resist uplift in this high-wind zone.

Details for a cedar eave

The home is T-shaped with two separate 5-pitch hip roofs separated by a 12-ft. section of flat roof. The building has 380 linear ft. of roof eave with one long, 64-ft. stretch. The trick is to install the rafter tails 24 in. apart and end up with a perfectly straight fascia board and eave line. The rafter tails are held down 7/8 in. from the top of the trusses so that cedar boards can be installed as the first layer of sheathing, exposing decorative cedar sheathing boards from below. With the top of the cedar boards now in plane with the top of the trusses, the bottom course of Zip System roof sheathing ties the 24-in. overhang and the roof trusses together.

NAIL 'EM ON. Fasten the first rafter tails near each corner of the roof and run a stringline between them. Use a piece of the cedar sheathing board as a gauge to set the top of each rafter tail 7/8 in. below the top of the truss and align the end of each rafter tail with the stringline.

SHIM TO PLUMB. Use a level to check each rafter tail to make sure it's installed plumb. If any need to be adjusted, use a pry bar and hammer to wedge shims between the truss and the rafter tail.

THE FIRST COURSE. Align the first course of cedar sheathing with the end of the rafter tails and fasten with two 8d stainless-steel ring-shank nails at each rafter.

ADD THE FASCIA. Use a 1x4 cedar fascia board installed flush with the top of the cedar sheathing boards, leaving the bottom of the rafter-tail face exposed.

START TIGHT. Even though they are kiln-dried, the cedar sheathing boards may move with changes in seasonal moisture. It's best to start with them tight to each other. A chisel is useful to pry the boards together before nailing.

CHEAP INSURANCE. Install a layer of #15 felt paper on top of the cedar sheathing boards so that if they do move and gaps open between them, the underside of the sheathing will not be visible from below.

TIE IT ALL TOGETHER. A full piece of Zip System sheathing ties the eaves to the trusses, adding plenty of strength to resist racking and uplift.

Shadowlines with purpose

Both the ventilation channel under the eaves and the boards to hold the metal drip edge away from the fascia provide opportunities to dress up the eave with even more shadowlines.

A PROTECTIVE DRIP EDGE. Add a 1x2 cedar board in plane with the roof sheathing to extend the drip edge away from the fascia, protecting it from excessive weathering.

HIDDEN VENTILATION. Install a black Cor-A-Vent strip to provide venting to the roof system and use stainless-steel finish nails to install the final pieces of cedar trim.

CUTTING CORNERS

THE HIP-RAFTER TAIL CATCHES both the back side and the bottom edges of the fascia boards to support the miter. With all the compound bevels, it takes some trial and error to cut the first piece. Start with all of the rafter tails installed along the length of the adjacent eaves and run the fascia boards to the miter at the corner. Then cut the first hip-rafter-tail profile with a coping saw and slide it into place beneath the fascia to test the fit. Once you have the first one fit, you can use it to make a template for the others.

CONTRIBUTORS

Jim Anderson is a framing contractor in Littleton, Colorado.

Rick Arnold is a builder and contributing editor to *Fine Homebuilding*.

Steve Baczek is an architect in Reading, Mass. Construction by Dunhill Builders, Osterville, Mass (dunhillbuilders.com).

Architect **Steve Baczek** and **Jim Wolffer** of Shoreline Builders have been collaborating on energy-smart, custom homes for over a decade.

Will Beemer is former coexecutive director of the Timber Framers Guild (www.tfguild.org) and director of the Heartwood School in Washington, Mass.

Paul Biebel is president of Biebel Builders, a design/build company in Windsor, Vt.

Don Burgard is a former *Fine Homebuilding* senior copy/ production editor.

Bill Cadley has run Pagoda Timber Frames in Chester, Conn., for more than 40 years.

Andy Engel is a former *Fine Homebuilding* editor. He learned to frame houses from several old-school carpenters.

Chris Ermides is a former *Fine Homebuilding* associate editor. Technical assistance from the staff at Structural Building Components Association.

Aaron Fagan is a former *Fine Homebuilding* copy/production editor.

Mike Guertin is a builder and remodeler in East Greenwich, R.I.

R. Bruce Hoadley is a former professor of wood science and technology at the University of Massachusetts at Amherst.

Paul Johnson and **Nathan D. Young** are building contractors based in Portland, Ore.

Gary M. Katz, former *Fine Homebuilding* contributing editor, is the driving force behind the Katz Roadshow and THISisCarpentry .com.

Danny Kelly of Kelly McArdle Construction is a homebuilder and remodeling contractor in Charlotte, N.C.

Sam Koerber is a custom builder in Asheville, N.C.

Patrick McCombe is senior editor of *Fine Homebuilding*.

Rob Munach, P.E., is a structural engineer. He operates Excel Engineering in Carrboro, N.C.

Mike Norton lives in Middleboro, Mass. His website is frametechs .com.

Roe A. Osborn, former *Fine Homebuilding* editor, is a freelance writer and photographer on Cape Cod, Mass.

Michael Patterson is a contractor in Gaithersburg, Md., and the president of the Metro DC chapter of the National Association of the Remodeling Industry (NARI).

Jud Peake is a member of carpenters union UBC Local 2236 and lives in Oakland, Calif.

Bryan Readling, P.E., is an engineer with APA-The Engineered Wood Association's Field Services Division in Davidson, N.C.

Debra Judge Silber is a former *Fine Homebuilding* managing editor.

John Spier is a builder on Block Island, R.I.

Michael Springer is a tool tester and tool-industry writer in Boulder County, Colo.

Brian Vogt is the carpentry department head at North Bennet Street School in Boston.

Rachel Wagner is a principal at Wagner Zaun Architecture (www.wagnerzaun.com) in Duluth, Minn.

Rob Yagid is former editor of *Fine Homebuilding*.

CREDITS

All photos are courtesy of *Fine Homebuilding* magazine (*FHB*) © The Taunton Press, Inc., except as noted below.

The articles in this book appeared in the following issues of *Fine Homebuilding*:

pp. 5–7: Building Skills: Outfitting a tool belt by Patrick McCombe, issue 225. Photos by Dan Thornton.

pp. 8–14: Choosing the Right Framing Nailer by Michael Springer, issue 230. Photos by Rodney Diaz, except for photo p. 9 by Justin Fink and inset product photos pp. 12–13 courtesy of Bostitch.

pp. 15–16: What's the Difference? Specialty levels by Don Burgard, issue 250. Photos by Rodney Diaz, except for photo p. 16 courtesy of iHandy.

pp. 17–22: Hammered by Aaron Fagan, issue 248. Photos by Rodney Diaz, except for inset photos pp. 18–19 courtesy of Jeffrey T. Cheney. Drawing by Bruce Morser.

pp. 23–25: How It Works: Nails by Debra Judge Silber, issue 245. Consultants: Douglas R. Rammer, USDA Forest Products Laboratory; Edward Sutt, Simpson Strong-Tie. Drawings by Christopher Mills.

pp. 26–27: What's the Difference? Framing lumber: Moisture content, species, and grade by Don Burgard, issue 222. Photo by Rodney Diaz.

pp. 28–29: What's the Difference? Pressure-treated lumber: Preserva- tives and retention by Don Burgard, issue 249. Photos by Rodney Diaz.

pp. 30–31: What's the Difference? Wooden scaffold planks: Solid-sawn vs. LVL by Don Burgard, issue 242. Photo p. 30 courtesy of ScaffoldMart.com, photo p. 31 courtesy of RedBuilt.

p. 33–39: 10 Golden Rules of Framing by Andy Engel, issue 270. Photos by *Fine Homebuilding* staff.

pp. 40–41: Letters: The next ten rules by John Spier, issue 272. Photos by Justin Fink.

pp. 42–43: How It Works: Simple wood beams by R. Bruce Hoadley, issue 258. Adapted from the revised edition of *Understanding Wood* by R. Bruce Hoadley (The Taunton Press, 2000). Drawings by Christo- pher Mills.

pp. 44–46: Building Skills: Cutting an acute bevel by Andy Engel, issue 257. Photos by Rodney Diaz.

pp. 47–53: Wind-Resistant Fram- ing Techniques by Bryan Readling, issue 237. Photos courtesy of Bryan Readling except for photos pp. 52–53 by Patrick McCombe. Drawings by Vince Babak.

pp. 54–55: How It Works: High winds vs. houses by Debra Judge Silber, issue 238. Sources: Insur- ance Institute for Business & Home Safety; National Wind Institute, Texas Tech University. Drawing by Christopher Mills.

pp. 56–60: The Precut Porch by Michael Patterson, issue 256. Photos by Michael Patterson except for photo p. 57 (bottom right) by Greg Hadley. Drawing by Michael Patterson.

pp. 61–63: Master Carpenter: Timber-framing joinery by Bill Cadley, issue 205. Photos by Charles Bickford except for photo p. 63 (bottom) courtesy of Makita.

pp. 64–69: Master Carpenter: The Essential Timber-Frame Joint by Will Beemer, issue 228. Photos by Charles Bickford except for p. 65 (top, bottom) by John Ross. Drawing by Dan Thornton.

pp. 70–76: Framing with a Crane by Jim Anderson, issue 140. Photos by Mike Rogers except for photo p. 71 by Andy Engel and bottom right photo p. 72, top photo p. 73, and top left photos p. 75 by Jim Anderson.

pp. 77–82: Bringing Advanced Framing to Your Job Site by Danny Kelly, issue 226. Photos by Patrick McCombe.

pp. 83–86: Framing for Efficiency by Steve Baczek, issue 244. Photos by Justin Fink. Drawing by John Hartman.

pp. 88–95: Exploring the Benefits of Engineered Floor Joists by Chris Ermides, issue 209. Product photos by Dan Thornton; photo p. 88 by Justin Fink; photo p. 91 (top) by Steve Culpepper; truss tags pp. 92–93 courtesy of Structural Build- ing Components Association and the Truss Plate Institute. Drawings pp. 92–93 by Bill Godfrey; drawings pp. 94–95 by Dan Thornton.

pp. 96–103: Build a Hybrid Timber-Frame Floor by Sam Koerber, issue 261. Photos by Justin Fink except for p. 96 by deborahscannell-photography.com, courtesy of Sam Koerber. Drawings by Christopher Mills.

pp. 104–111: Fast, Accurate Floor Sheathing by Danny Kelly, issue 229. Photos by Patrick McCombe. Drawing by Don Mannes.

pp. 113–115: How It Works: Wall framing by Rob Munach, issue 214. Photo by Daniel S. Morrison. Drawing by Don Mannes.

pp. 116–123: Fast and Accurate Wall Framing by Mike Norton, issue 242. Photos by Charles Bickford.

pp. 124–131: Frame a Gable Wall by Brian Vogt, issue 272. Photos by Patrick McCombe. Drawing by Rodney Diaz.

pp. 132–134: Building Skills: Installing a big beam by Andy Engel, issue 254. Photos by Justin Fink except for product photos p. 134 by Dan Thornton.

pp. 135–141: The Right Header for Every Wall by Mike Guertin, issue 264. Photos courtesy of Mike Guertin except for photos p. 139 by Dan Thornton. Drawings by Don Mannes.

pp. 142–144: Building Skills: Laying out stud walls by Andy Engel, issue 274. Photos and drawings by Rodney Diaz.

pp. 145–147: Energy Smart Details: Double-stud walls by Rachel Wagner, issue 228. Drawings by Elden Lindamood, courtesy of Wagner Zaun Architecture.

pp. 148–152: Air-sealed Mudsill Assembly by Steve Baczek, issue 241. Photos by Justin Fink except for product photos p. 150 and p. 152 by Dan Thornton. Drawing by John Hartman.

pp. 153–154: How It Works: Shear walls by Rob Yagid, issue 222. Drawings by Don Mannes.

pp. 155–158: A Slick Approach to Straightening Walls by Roe A. Osborn, issue 214. Adapted from *Framing a House* (The Taunton Press, 2010). Photos by Roe A. Osborn. Photo illustration p. 156 by Bill Godfrey.

pp. 159–165: Bringing Back Balloon-Frame Construction by Paul Biebel, issue 260. Photos by Paul Biebel. Drawings by Christopher Mills.

pp. 167–169: Building Skills: Laying out and cutting common rafters by Andy Engel, issue 265. Photos and drawing by Rodney Diaz.

pp. 170–174: Perfect Roof Rafters by Sam Koerber, issue 256. Photos by Justin Fink. Drawings by Don Mannes.

pp. 175–179: Building Craftsman-Style Brackets by Gary M. Katz, issue 238. Photos by Gary M. Katz. Drawings by John Hartman.

pp. 180–181: How It Works: Collar and rafter ties by Debra Judge Silber, issue 240. Drawings by Christopher Mills.

pp. 182–186: Master Carpenter: Framing an octagonal turret roof by Rick Arnold, issue 224. Photos by John Ross except for photo p. 186 (bottom) courtesy of Big Foot Tools. Drawings by Rodney Diaz.

pp. 187–192: Frame a Classic Shed Dormer by John Spier, issue 200. Photos by Justin Fink. Drawings by Dan Thornton.

pp. 193–195: Master Carpenter: Three ways to lay out an elliptical curve by Jud Peake, issue 214. Main photo p. 193 courtesy of Architectural Resources Group Inc.; inset photo p. 193 by David Wakely. Drawings by Rodney Diaz.

pp. 196–197: How It Works: Roof trusses by Rob Munach, issue 225. Drawings by Toby Welles/ WowHouse.

pp. 198–204: Framing Tricky Truss Roofs by Paul Johnson and Nathan D. Young, issue 225. Photos by Patrick McCombe except photos p. 198, pp. 200-201 (main), and p. 203 by Nina Johnson. Drawings by Don Mannes.

pp. 205–210: Elegant Eaves for a Truss Roof by Steve Baczek and Jim Wolffer, issue 277. Photos by Brian Pontolilo. Drawings by John Hartman.

INDEX